MW00778460

BUILDING
BRANDS

&

CREATING
CULTURES

OF AUTHENTIC SERVANT LEADERSHIP

4TH DIMENSION LEADERSHIP SERIES

STACY WALL SCHWEIKHART
WITH INSIGHTS FROM RON HOLIFIELD

Published by BookLocker.com, Inc., St. Petersburg, Florida.

Printed on acid-free paper.

BookLocker.com, Inc.
2018

First Edition

DISCLAIMER

This book details the author's personal experiences and opinions about leadership.

The author and publisher are providing this book and its contents on an "as is" basis and make no representations or warranties of any kind with respect to this book or its contents. The author and publisher disclaim all such representations and warranties, including for example warranties of merchantability and HR advice for a particular purpose. In addition, the author and publisher do not represent or warrant that the information accessible via this book is accurate, complete or current.

The statements made about products and services have not been evaluated by the U.S. government. Please consult with your own legal or HR professional regarding the suggestions and recommendations made in this book.

Except as specifically stated in this book, neither the authors or publisher, nor any authors, contributors, or other representatives will be liable for damages arising out of or in connection with the use of this book. This is a comprehensive limitation of liability that applies to all damages of any kind, including (without limitation) compensatory; direct, indirect or consequential damages; loss of data, income or profit; loss of or damage to property and claims of third parties.

You understand that this book is not intended as a substitute for consultation with a licensed legal or human resources professional.

This book provides content related to leadership topics. As such, use of this book implies your acceptance of this disclaimer.

my true north

Table of Contents

Prologue

As a college student at the University of Dayton I serendipitously found my way in to an experiential learning course called "Leadership in Building Communities". Taught by the then President of the University Brother Ray Fitz and two members of his team, Don Vermillion and Dick Ferguson, the course paired students with urban neighborhoods to complete an asset map and an action plan for desired improvements.

The entire course was built on the foundation of servant leadership and the teachings of Robert K. Greenleaf. We learned by the example to engage side by side with the community, not to sweep in and do something FOR them. We learned to facilitate constructive conversations. We learned that the key to sustaining change is authentic relationships. We learned that true leaders have heart, not necessarily titles.

That course changed my life. A psychology major with plans to go to law school, I started shifting my path toward public service. Deep within, I felt a call to work to better communities. I felt a burden to help close the gap I perceived between where communities and organizations could be and where they are. In every role I've held since, servant leadership has been at the core of my why.

The experience also blessed me with a career mentor in Don Vermillion. He was the ultimate servant leader in each and every sense of the term. A former city manager and county administrator, Don "retired" and dedicated the rest of his life to illuminating the path to public service for students and young professionals. Look around the Dayton region and it is hard to find a public serving organization without leaders who were in some way students or mentees inspired by Don.

Fast forward a decade or so. I attended one of Ron's presentations and the underlying servant leadership message resonated deeply. Over the years that followed, Ron & I had several conversations about the changing demands of organizational leadership and our common belief that though the pressure is growing the answer is still the same.

Your people and your culture will determine your ability to thrive in spite of the challenges.

When Ron released "4th Dimension Leadership" in 2017, I found myself immersed in the compelling challenge he laid out. I filled the margins of the book with notes, questions and observations.

When Ron exalted the need for all systems within an organization to align to build a servant leader culture, I wrote in the margin **Yes,** followed by **but do organizations know how?**.

I was blown away, and deeply honored, when Ron asked if I would consider writing the next book in the SGR 4th Dimension Leadership series. A book that would attempt to answer many of the questions I wrote in the margins as I read his book.

I might as well get this confession out of the way. Ron did not ask me to write this book on branding and culture because I hold advanced degrees from a pedigree marketing or communication program. So if what you are looking for is pure, unadulterated branding advice, this is not the book for you. This is definitively not a marketing book.

If, on the other hand, your primary motivation is to deepen your commitment to being a servant leader, and to understand the critical actions you can take to shape systems within your organization to instill a servant leadership culture, read on. If you are called to build community, both within your organization and those you serve – read on.

This is not a "you should" book. If you are looking for why "you should" and you haven't read Ron's 4th Dimension Leadership book yet, start there.

Until now the common way to get from "you should" to action involved hiring a consultant or bobbling your way through semi-blind with mixed results.

This book is the next step in the process.

It is built around the same foundation from Greenleaf that Ron cites in 4th Dimension Leadership - that the twelve characteristic of Servant Leadership are:

- Listening
- Empathy
- Healing
- Nurturing the spirit
- Building community
- Awareness
- Foresight
- Conceptualization
- Persuasion
- Calling
- Stewardship
- Commitment to the growth of people

This is truly a "how to" book. If you come along with me on this journey, you will be on the path to building a brand and creating a culture of authentic servant leadership.

I'm one of you. I believe in this stuff. If only one organization can use this roadmap to implement a shift toward a servant leadership culture my mission is accomplished.

I know the impact it will have on hearts of your team and I am confident that it will shift the soul of your organization for the good of the people you serve.

Think of this book as a guide to establishing your own road map. I will walk you through figuring out where your journey must begin and where you'd like it to end. I'll make sure to point out critical parts of the path and potential stumbling points along the way. I'll give you some suggestions that might make the journey more meaningful. I'll even give you a heads up about places where you might encounter a traffic jam or a detour.

Just like a family road trip, there is one rule. No asking "are we there yet". I assure you that when you get there, and even when you're on the right road along the way, you'll know it. More importantly, there is no way to estimate how long this road trip will take. Take your time and enjoy the journey!

INSIGHTS FROM RON

When I first began deeply studying organizational culture as part of my research in writing 4th Dimension Leadership – Radical Strategies for Creating an Authentic Servant Leadership Culture, I was honestly surprised at what I learned regarding the interconnectedness between culture and brand reputation. And the more I learned, the more I realized how much I did not know. I discovered that for me (and probably for you) the entire concept of brand management was more than a bit of a blind spot when focusing on creating the type of sustainable culture we desired.

As a result, I began searching for an expert who not only understood brand management, but also understood local government and authentically bought in to servant leadership principles. I went in search of someone who could help fill the critical gap in practical understanding of how to successfully manage your brand from a culture perspective because I knew I did not have that expertise.

I had heard Stacy speak at other conferences, and as a result asked her to speak at the SGR Servant Leadership Conference on brand management. After hearing her speak at the SGR Servant Leadership Conference, I knew I had found the right expert and immediately urged her to do a book on the subject. Stacy brings the expertise that I (and most of us) lack in the practical strategies needed to manage a brand. But she also brings a wealth of experience in media relations, crisis communications, and community relations, as well as branding and culture.

But most significantly, Stacy has studied, believes in, and walks the talk of authentic servant leadership.

The fact that Stacy "gets it" has been demonstrated in her being tapped repeatedly to serve in leadership roles with various regional, state and national associations and organizations. Stacy has a national reputation in local government circles and is clearly a thought leader when it comes to managing your brand reputation. I have learned much from her in the process of assisting her in the development of this book. I am confident you also will learn much from her about how to manage your brand in a way that helps you create an authentic servant leadership culture just as I have.

We have been conditioned to equate building a brand with marketing. But marketing is what you do to accomplish audience specific goals, while your brand is who you are (or at least who others perceive that you are!).

Let that sink in for a moment.

Your brand is your identity... it is how others see you.

Your brand can be positive or negative, accurate or inaccurate, but the impact that your brand has on your success is profound...

far too important to be left to chance.

Unfortunately, that is exactly what most organizations do – they leave their brand identity to chance by failing to understand (and then act upon) the ways they can positively build their brand.

Behavioral norms create authentic culture, and your authentic culture determines your brand reputation.

Culture is simply the behavioral norms of your employees -- and those behavioral norms determine how those you serve are treated each time an interaction occurs.

In the case of local government, a typical citizen only has a significant interaction with your organization about once every two years. Yet every time an employee interacts with someone you serve, your brand reputation is being shaped in a way that will define your brand in the mind of that person for a long time to come. Each, and every personal interaction is an "aha moment" which has a disproportionate impact on how that person will define your brand. In doing so, you shape expectations regarding the type and quality of services you provide, and then people tend to demand that their expectations be met.

As the organization becomes conditioned to meet those expectations (both positive and negative), behavioral norms are established, and those norms define the authentic culture and brand identity of an organization regardless of what posters you have on the wall claiming it is.

Think about a closed loop... your brand reputation shapes expectations of those you serve...which shapes team performance... which shapes your reputation.

Your brand is shaped most by interaction.

Think about a typical driver's license bureau and the last time you went to get your driver's license renewed. You likely put it off until the last minute because you anticipated what a negative experience it was going to be.

When you arrived, there was a mass of people already in an unbelievably slow-moving line, the design and furnishings of the room felt like something out of the 1950's, there were not enough clerks to handle the number of people, and the clerks that were there reminded you of the teacher in Ferris Buehler's Day off dripping with slow moving boredom as he called out "Buehler, Buehler".

That may or may not be a fair or accurate reflection of reality, but it is the real brand reputation that too many drivers' license bureaus live with.

In Texas, I am only required to go in person to get my driver's license renewed once every 8 years. But my interaction from "the last time" still shapes my dread of doing it again a full 8 years later! Interaction (positive or negative) has a profound impact on how we interpret the brand of organizations we deal with and once formed, those impressions are hard to overcome.

Your brand creates self-fulfilling expectations of both current and future individuals you serve.

I worked with one community whose elected officials value low taxes above all else and are willing to sacrifice quality of services for the lowest possible tax rate.

At the same time, I worked with another community who considered excellence in both the array of services offered and the quality of those services to be a priority and are willing to pay for excellence.

It is not hard to predict, that the type of residents who move to the first community tend to tolerate mediocre services, while the type of residents who move to the second one expect excellence and are willing to pay for it.

And predictably, the community with a commitment to excellence maintains higher property values, which drives up home prices because demand for a home in the second community is higher, which means that the people who move there expect quality services and are willing to pay for it.

In other words, your brand reputation tends to create more of what you are known for.

Your brand shapes your candidate pools.

This is one of the most often missed aspects of the importance of brand management.

One city I work with can simply post an ad on their state municipal league job board and they will have an overflowing pool of high quality candidates aspiring to work for them.

An adjacent city which I also work with can spend tens of thousands of dollars on recruitment marketing and struggle to have an acceptable candidate pool. Both cities are about the same size and complexity and both pay about the same.

What creates such a profound difference in the candidate pools?

Brand reputation.

Your brand doesn't just determine who wants to live in your community; it determines who wants to work for your organization.

A mediocre brand produces mediocre candidate pools. Mediocre candidate pools produce mediocre behavioral norms, which produces a mediocre performance culture. A mediocre culture produces mediocre brand reputation.

It is a vicious circle which can be very difficult to break out of.

Your brand helps you deal with internet trolls and political dysfunction.

We are in a new world in which many of the old rules no longer apply.

A significant problem in discourse and decision making in communities and organizations today is the amount of information, and especially inaccurate information that is shaping opinions and attitudes.

In fact, we are drowning in information which can create dramatic challenges to community decision making.

Gloria Origgi in Fast Company magazine has written that "We are experiencing a fundamental paradigm shift in our relationship to knowledge from an 'information age', we are moving towards the 'reputation age' in which information will have value only if it is already filtered, evaluated and commented on by others.

Seen in this light, reputation has become a central pillar of collective intelligence today." Origgi goes on to say that "The paradigm shift from the age of information to the age of reputation must be taken into account when we try to defend ourselves against fake news and other misinformation and disinformation techniques that are proliferating through contemporary societies.

What a mature consumer in the digital age should be competent at is not spotting and confirming the veracity of the news.

Rather she should be competent at reconstructing the reputational path of the piece of information in question, evaluating the intentions of those who circulated it, and figuring out the agendas of those authorities that leant it credibility."

In other words... your brand reputation will determine how credible you are.

Your brand reputation will determine the type and expectations of individuals and businesses who will move to your community, seek out your service or purchase your product; their attitude and expectations once they become a part of your community; the type of candidate pools you have to choose from; and your very credibility in your own community or organization.

Building your brand must not be a side function of your Marketing, Community Relations or Public Information office.

If you are to control your destiny in today's world, building your brand must be a core responsibility of the entire organization, but especially of senior leadership.

This book provides you with a practical roadmap for building a brand and creating a culture of authentic servant leadership.

Stacy is going to walk you through the process of creating a roadmap.

My job is to share some insights along the way.

Throughout you can look for my real world bumps, bruises and best ideas in boxes just like this one.

Let's start the journey!

Ron

Part One:
Building a Brand

Chapter 1:
Brand Basics

Imagine this: It's Saturday morning. You head to your local grocery store armed with your list of needed items. You peruse aisle to aisle quickly picking up supplies for the week. The trip is faster than normal because there are few decisions. The laundry detergent all looks essentially the same. The yogurt aisle is far less overwhelming. The cereal aisle is a quarter of its normal length.

Or is that really how it would go? Maybe instead the trip takes far longer than normal. How are you supposed to know which laundry detergent to buy?!? They all look the same!

You see, you are shopping in a time before brand identity invaded the marketplace.

The birth of brand marketing happened as consumer companies rapidly entered the marketplace and sought a way to help shoppers identify and select their product or service for purchase. It started with the color and shape of the packaging or signage, then distinct brand logos. Then of course the incorporation of brand messaging into broadcast commercials and print advertising.

Branding gives an identity to an otherwise generic product or service.

Brand identity is the reason you can quickly find your favorite products on the store shelves. Brand messaging is the sales hook that gets you to try a product for the first time. Brand positioning is the flashy end cap that slides the money right out of my wallet more often than I'd care to admit.

Whew! Two pages in and for the non-marketing professional I've already thrown out some jargon. Let me break down the marketing side of branding for you. I promise this lesson won't be too terribly overwhelming.

Brand identity

Brand identity is the simplified, readily identifiable visual representation of your brand. Yes, in most cases this is your logo. But there are other aspects of brand identity like your signature colors, the shape of your signage or packaging. This can even include the font you use.

Brand messaging

Brand messaging is what most will recognize as taglines. That second line behind the title of your product or service that tells more about them. If done well, this is the hook, the memorable jingle. The sales pitch, the phrase that connects with consumers.

Brand voice

Brand voice is the clear tone and personality of your product or service. Establishing your voice helps you to relate to the audience you are trying to reach. Who is your brand persona?

Brand positioning

Unless you've really hit the jackpot, which probably means you have a late night infomercial, you aren't the only product or service in your consumer category. Who are you in your consumer market?

Brand standards

To most, this is the boring part, but it is critical. This is where a style guide comes in. Brand standards include key distinctive features like your font, your specific colors, your acceptable logo orientations, your design themes for promotional pieces. This is the very technical part of your brand identity.

Brand placement

Where you choose to place your brand matters. The products or services you align your organization with contribute to the creation of your identity. The easiest example is that an organization who wants to be seen as forward thinking probably shouldn't slap their logo and marketing materials on a CD to promote their community. At least use a USB drive. Even better put your logo and link to website containing all the marketing materials on a USB charging cord. My golden rule is to always thoughtfully match brand placement with purpose.

Brand priorities

What is your brand seeking to do? How do all of the other components of your brand align to do this? Let's be clear – this can change as your priorities change and as the market changes.

Brand consistency

As far as I'm concerned, consistency is the golden rule of branding. There is no more certain doom for a brand than one that lacks consistency. That means consistency on the marketing side of course, but more critically it means consistency on the product or service delivery side. It means you have a reliable brand that consumers know they can count on.

Please allow me to pull out my soapbox for a moment. Now that I have covered some of the elements from the marketing side of a brand, it's also critical that you recognize what your brand is not.

Your brand is not your logo. It is not your signature color, no matter how many pieces of logoed apparel in this color you give your team. It's not the slightly Stepford way all of your employees incorporate your signature color in to their personal wardrobes or wear your fancy logo pins. It is not your slick website; your social media account graphics; your hip business cards.

These things are brand elements and marketing. Indeed it may be marketing that uses your brand identity, but it is not your brand.

Your brand is how those you serve perceive you.

For better or worse, your brand carries the perception of your product or service. For better or worse! Certainly we can all think of a few great examples in both of these categories.

This is a book about servant leadership culture. Why in the world are you talking about branding?!? Trust me, they are intrinsically connected and your ability to build not just a strong servant leader culture, but also a productive and meaningful one, depends first on your ability to crystalize your brand - both internally and externally.

As public servants, non-profit leaders, health care executives or progressive business professionals we strive to develop a strong servant leadership culture. To do what? To deliver your products and services to the people you serve. Ultimately that is why we are here.

Trust me. This book is not about marketing. It is about truly understanding your brand so that you can refine it in order to create a servant leadership culture. Going through the exercises outlined in the next several chapters will help you build a more authentic, purposeful servant leadership culture.

INSIGHTS FROM RON

It is not a coincidence that organizations who manage their brand, tend to have the best reputation!

The City of Plano is one of the best examples in the nation of an organization who knows who they are and manages their brand reputation exceptionally well in both the large and the small things. Their tag line "City of Excellence" really does define how they see themselves and it permeates their conversations when they are talking about citizen expectations.

Early in my career, I worked as an Assistant City Manager in Plano. Frito Lay had recently relocated its' headquarters from Dallas to Plano, but their millions and millions of products sold all over the world still reflected Dallas as their home. The City understood that helping Plano become known internationally as a corporate headquarters community contributed to recruiting additional corporate headquarters, as well as helping shape the self-perception of their own citizens and employees.

It took two years for the change to take place, but today the back of every single Frito Lay product that goes out across the globe identifies Plano as the home of Frito Lay.

I know having your community name on the back of a consumer product can sound like a small thing (indeed the print on the back of each bag IS small)... but that is sort of the point. To do successful brand management means managing everything that can shape your identity and your reputation. To do it well is to do it holistically.

Get ready for Stacy to provide you a "paint by number" process to help you do exactly that.

Chapter 2:
Your External Brand

For the purposes of this chapter, when I speak of your brand please think of the external perception of your organization or who you are in the eyes of the outside world. In the realm of the public sector, this is the way those you serve perceive your city, your county, township, hospital system, library system, non-profit organization, airport or special district. Yes, even if all your organization has is an ancient logo originally created before I was born – you have a brand.

As marketing teams seek to establish an identity for their brand, they identify the key characteristics and defining attributes they want their brand to represent.

For organizations, particularly for those who are public serving, it is the set of human characteristics that those you serve identify when they think of you.

This exercise is critical. It provides a strong foundation upon which the future success of your brand and furthermore your culture are built.

Disclaimer: This process does not require a marketing firm, a PR professional or a robust budget. In fact I have been known, much to the dismay of fellow presenters at conference sessions, to BEG attendees in my sessions not to use a consultant to lead this process.

Why? It's simple. Your brand identity - your logo, your marketing templates, your web design - can be bought.

But your organization's brand and your culture can not be bought. They can only be grown, day in and day out with each interaction that occurs amongst your employees and those that occur between your employees and the public.

Here's the critical reason above and beyond all else. If you hire a consultant or a third party to lead this and you have just told your team that none of them have the capacity to do it. And you've told them that you don't have the capacity or the courage to do it.

This process is, and should be, personal.

Culture is personal.

Ideally, in order to demonstrate the commitment to establishing servant leadership culture as Ron describes in 4th Dimension the process should be supported and facilitated from the top. If not the top administrator, someone very close to her level of authority and influence.

By all means, seeking out an advisor like me or Ron or another expert to support your efforts may be worthwhile. But only you can lead the shift to a servant leadership culture for your organization.

EXERCISE 1:
WHAT IS YOUR DESIRED BRAND?

This is easy. How do you want those you serve to perceive you? And by easy I mean easy in theory. In reality, this part may be as painful as those all day sessions to come up with an organizational mission and vision.

Let's go back to the idea that a brand creates an identity for your product or service. Or in this case an identity for your organization, your realm of public service. This identity is created by establishing some key characteristics and attributes people think of when they think of your organization.

You can approach determining your desired brand in several ways and the right way largely depends on your organization. Some organizations, though few, are veterans to considering their brand. For others this is a brand new world.

This is easy, but it is also easy to fall off course. Here's why: Too many organizations insert buzz words here thinking that is the sure way to succeed. Perfect example? Excellence.

I've seen it a million times in organizational mission statements and aspirational strategic plans. The problem? What does excellence look like and what does it mean to the people you serve? The average person does not think of any brand and immediately say - Excellence! To me, it is a prime example of a meaningless and impossible to measure term when used to describe a desired brand. Which means this process is over before it even started.

This doesn't mean that using a term like "excellence" in your slogans or messaging is a mistake. The example Ron cited from Plano is a perfect example of how it can work. But it worked because Plano was deeply committed to demonstrating the meaning of the term, not just using it in an empty attempt to convey value.

My best advice is for you and your team to use human characteristics and attributes when you seek to describe your desired brand, not business buzz words. Remember the qualities of servant leaders: empathetic, nurturing, forward-thinking, invested in people.

Now that you have an idea of what your team will be asked to accomplish, it is time to thoughtfully assemble a group of advisors who have demonstrated a commitment to improving culture and acting as leaders in your organization.

STEP 1: WHO ARE THE ADVISORS?

A sneak peek into future exercises: this core team is absolutely critical and will be the foundation of significant work in future exercises. Take the time to carefully build this team right the first time. Seek representation from a broad cross section of your organization. I would strongly caution you against accepting core team members who are assigned by their supervisors without true buy-in. Instead, solicit and recruit individuals who have a passion for their work and your organization, and who have earned the consistent respect of their colleagues.

A certain reality in public serving organizations is that you need to include your board or directors, stakeholders or elected officials in this process. How they expect the organization they lead to be perceived is critical. Here's the other thing: Once you determine how those you serve perceive your organization and move forward with any measures necessary to bridge the gap between where you truly are and where you want to be, you are going to need their buy in. They are critical actors, and the ultimate ambassadors for your organization.

I'd also dare to say that this is a perfect opportunity to involve up and coming leaders in your organization. A wide cross section of position types, management levels and career stages is critical in the group you assemble.

Diversity of thought at the internal level in the early stages of this process will reap rewards later. Not to mention that involvement breeds ownership, a dimension that will become critical as the forthcoming stages of this process evolve.

I'd like to offer a concept for your consideration as you assemble this team.

LEADERSHIP VORTEX

This brings me to one of my favorite stories. In fact, I've built a full on-site organizational training known as Leadership Vortex with this story as the centerpiece. This of course is a much abbreviated version.

My sons both attend a Montessori school. During a parent conference their teacher described a critical part of the teaching method. I recount it as follows:

The teacher offers a lesson on a particular topic. Built in to the lesson are opportunities for students to complete a basic level of interactive work or for those who are interested to delve more fully into intense study and demonstration of the concept.

Some students select the very minimal basic level of work. Some become immersed. Both are ok.

By nature the Montessori classroom allows this type of freedom for students to gravitate toward work that interests them. Engagement varies widely from student to student, and even for the same student according to the topic of the lesson.

The teacher's job then is to pay attention to which students become immersed in which topics and to the overall pattern of engagement for each student.

The day after the parent teacher conferences a light bulb went off.

What if organizational leaders crafted a similar experience for their teams?

What if supervisors and managers paid more attention to the patterns of engagement for each employee?

What might that reveal about the employee, the team and the organization as a whole?

Like I said - those answers are a workshop on their own.

The scaled down theory that is relevant to this book is the idea that certain employees consistently contribute and reliably engage regardless of the project. Without another way to accurately describe it, they just get it.

These are the people you want working on this process. Find a handful of them in your organization and hold on tight!

Likewise, there are plenty in every organization who will do the absolute minimum to check the box. Who will spin around the top of the vortex, not exerting more energy or devoting more effort than absolutely necessary? Often, they have made their way to management and leadership roles in your organization by seniority or default. They are not the people you want involved in this process. They will weigh you down and put the entire effort at risk.

STEP 2: FACILITATING THE FEEDBACK

Face-to-face meetings are probably best. This is my default because I think they are the most authentic and they lend themselves to the most revealing conversations. Yes, they take a lot of time. Yes, there can be serious divergence of thought. Yes, it is worth it.

A relevant aside on the theme of servant leadership:

A true servant leader knows that constructive conversations are at the heart of gaining trust and establishing relationships. Constructive conversations can be tumultuous, but are also the most rewarding. Your role as a servant leader is to use your influence to guide discussions, often full of contrary perspectives, to a meaningful result all involved can adopt as their own. Certainly leading the exercises outlined in this book will require some constructive conversations.

Now the method to orchestrate these meetings is really up to the facilitator. Really any style with a proven track record for successful results in your organization and your community will work.

Get started by explaining the purpose. The purpose is to identify how our organization wants those we serve to think of us and to form a collective aspirational perception.

STEP 3: THE LIST

What you are going for is a crisp, meaningful set of human characteristics, descriptors or attributes.

You want at least three and no more than 7 characteristics.

There is no one set of characteristics that fit all organizations. The attributes you choose should be as unique to your organization and your constituents as possible.

Some things to consider:

What are your long range strategic goals?

What are your short term and long term challenges?

What are your greatest success?

What are your most valuable assets?

Who are you trying to attract to your community, your organization or your services?

Now - what are the attributes that best describe the way your organization needs to be perceived in order to attain these goals or continue the successes?

A common and natural pitfall at this point in the process is to start making a list of perceived current deficits or challenges. For the time being, place the known struggles aside. There will be plenty of time later to assess current brand. Focus on truly aspirational, servant leader aligned characteristics.

Once you have this accomplished – which may take one meeting or six – you are ready to move on to the next step to determine your current brand.

EXERCISE 2:
DETERMINING YOUR CURRENT BRAND

Now that you know how you hope those you serve perceive you, let's find out what they think of you right now.

This is your brand – even if it isn't one you are thrilled to own.

There are several ways to accomplish this. The most important thing to remember is that this is not something you can identify without talking to your customers, your community.

For most organizations, determining your current external brand is best accomplished by including questions about your brand in a community or user survey. But what questions do you ask? And how?

STEP 1: DECIDE WHAT TO ASK

This is where the work of your internal team in Exercise 1 comes in. Include in the survey the crisp, meaningful attributes they agreed upon as your desired brand.

Here's the kicker. You have to put some characteristics on the survey that aren't all hearts & flowers. Meaning, if you know there are some unfavorable connotations out there, or could be, don't bury your head in the sand. If there are areas where you know your organization is missing the mark on servant leadership, put them on the list.

Don't go through this exercise unless you are willing to do it authentically. It's a waste of your time, your staff's time, your community's time and it risks some serious damage to whatever brand you have if the list you put out only included gold star characteristics. Take a deep breath and be willing to find out what your community really thinks of your brand.

So your community survey could be as simple as this:

Please circle five of the following attributes you feel best describe us.

Honest

Empathetic

Hard working

Transparent

Trustworthy

High Quality

Reliable

Fun

Warm

Covert

Innovative

Dedicated

Responsible

Out of Touch

Dishonest

Service-oriented

Lazy

Caring

In-demand

Unreliable

Approachable

Inconsistent

Acceptable

Stale

Cutting Edge

Confusing

Aware

Difficult

Accessible

Ineffective

Elitist

Wasteful

Resourceful

Friendly

Rude

Forward thinking

Thriving

Good Stewards

Declining

STEP 2: SURVEY METHODS

This can be executed one of the old fashioned ways – in person, by phone or direct mail. It could be a great project for a graduate student*, management intern, an up & coming high potential employee or a team of volunteers.

*side note: as a bonus for any organization that brings on a graduate student intern to guide this project I will make myself available to them for any guidance I can provide. I am willing to do this because I believe wholeheartedly in offering real, meaningful experiences for bright young people entering the field of public service.

I'm a fan of using a robust e-mail database and sending a message that includes a link to an online survey. The database you use should be as closely related to a service used by all of your audience as possible. In the public sector world, think utility service or trash. All of your audience means all of those who could potentially access your services, not just your frequent fliers or those who are already patients, customers, members or donors.

I like online survey platforms like SurveyMonkey, because they do the tabulation and graphics for you. There are also tons of tech companies out there who offer survey capabilities as part of more broad engagement platforms. As is my standard stance, they are great but they are not as cost effective as the simple free tools that will do the job just as well.

Certainly you could post the link to the survey on your social media accounts. The value of this method depends largely on the amount of followers you have on those accounts, the average representative reach of your posts and the proportion of your account followers who actually represent your audience. Any time you post a survey for the entire world to see, you risk responses from those outside your audience.

You also risk an attack by trolls. Oh how we know them well. No one can submarine survey results faster than a troll or team of trolls. Limit this as much as possible by setting up your online survey to only allow one response per IP address. Also pay attention to the clever language and key phrases that trolls hold so dear. You'll likely be able to identify if you've fallen victim to a coordinated attack.

Regardless of your method, for the results to be valuable you must ensure that the respondents represent a large cross section of those you serve. This point may seem a little remedial, but you wouldn't do 100% of your surveys on the sidelines of a preschool soccer game or at the senior center just like you shouldn't do 100% of your surveys on social media. Both would limit the demographics of your respondents and lead to skewed results that aren't a true representation of the way your organization is perceived.

Let's talk about representative sample size since we are on the topic. It is worth your time to calculate the total population you'd like to measure, the confidence level you want to achieve and the amount of variance you are comfortable with tolerating. For the non-statistician, here's what I mean. If the population you serve is 5,000 people, you need 357 completed surveys to say within +/-5 point variance that your results are 95% accurate. Google is your friend. Search for a representative sample size calculator and use it.

STEP 3: EVALUATING THE RESULTS

You've collected your surveys. Now simply tabulate the most frequent responses. This isn't the end all, be all definition of your brand. But it is a great start, particularly if you've never created a baseline to understand what those you serve think of you.

Hopefully, the most common responses are positive. Hopefully they are consistent with the perception you want those you serve to have of you.

If they are – fist bump! Either intentionally or accidentally, you are doing something right. In this case, it may be worth it to follow up in the near future with an effort to gather insight into why your audience perceives you the way they do. What are the key programs, services or commitments that solidify these perceptions? More importantly, what are the key components of employee interactions with those you serve that lead to this perception?

What if the results aren't exactly what you hoped they would be? Welcome to the club.

True story, when we first conducted this survey for the organization where I work one of the descriptors with a high percentage of responses was "acceptable".

This can be worrisome, but believe me it is not uncommon. But as the wise ones say, it is what it is. At least you know and can move forward to do something about it.

In Chapter 5 we will start to examine ways to close the gap. But first, a little insight from Ron and then there's another angle we need to explore.

INSIGHTS FROM RON

We are in an era in which individuals are increasingly disconnecting from institutions of all kinds. Never before in history have we been so networked and so disconnected at the same time.

Whether it is the type of toothpaste used, the brand of car driven, or the religious institution attended – the norm today is that people will switch loyalty at the drop of a hat. While they cannot change which city they live in on a whim... this same lack of institutional loyalty towards their home community is playing out in different ways.

There is often a higher sense of affiliation with a neighborhood or homeowner's association than with the city they live in. In fact, one city I worked with conducted a survey of their citizens and found that 20% of their citizens did not even know what city they lived in! Let that sink in. How do you manage your brand reputation with your citizens if they do not even realize that they live in your city?

In this increasingly disconnected environment, learning what your brand reputation really is out in the community is more important than ever before – and more challenging to figure out.

But knowing and understanding what your real brand reputation is, is only the first step. Managing your brand when it comes to customer interactions is where the greatest opportunity for either reinforcing or changing your brand reputation. Every single interaction is a reflection of the authentic values and culture of the organization. Not a reflection of the words you have on the wall somewhere, but of the real honest to goodness behavioral norms that are your real culture.

Almost a decade ago, my Keurig coffee maker went on the blink. I went to their website to try and find out about the warranty. I found a phone number and called it. The friendly voice on the other end looked it up and apologized that it was out of warranty. I told her that was okay, that I would just toss it and go purchase a new one, to which she responded, "Oh no need to do that, I will send you a new one. It will go out today and you should have it by Monday." I was completely caught off guard by the amazing customer service.

I learned a lot about their customer centric culture and in that interaction. It made me feel like they authentically cared, and that they walked their talk of caring with an action-oriented commitment to real solutions. Over a decade later, not only am I still drinking Keurig coffee... I am still telling people about what an awesome customer service experience that one interaction was!

The single most important thing you can do to manage your external brand is to deliver customer experiences that authentically walk the talk of the culture you claim to have. But to do that, you have to begin with managing your internal brand. Stacy is going to show you how to do that next.

Chapter Three:
Your Internal Brand

Consider the exercises in Chapter 2 your warm up.

Certainly your external brand matters. But quite frankly if that were your primary concern I doubt you'd be reading a book with servant leadership as a foundation. Instead you'd be reading mass market branding advice and trying to apply it to your organization. Or even more likely you would be hiring marketing experts to do it for you.

Because you are going at this branding & culture stuff with an interest in servant leadership, you may already understand why determining your internal brand is the critical next step.

For the purposes of this chapter, when I speak of your internal brand please think of the perception those within your organization have of the organization as a whole. Not the perception they have of the head honcho, or any particular co-worker, or their support of any of your board members or elected officials. Internal brand is how they as individuals think overall about your organization, particularly as it relates to them personally.

What you are about to read will sound very familiar. Essentially, you are going to repeat the process of determining your external brand using the same exercises, just with an inward focus.

Just as you did as you determined your external brand, the next step is to identify the key characteristics, descriptors and defining attributes you want your internal brand to reflect.

This exercise is critical. It provides a strong foundation upon which the future success of your entire brand and your organizational culture are built.

The disclaimer from Chapter 2 is worth repeating:

This process does not require a marketing firm, a PR professional or a robust budget. Ideally, in order to demonstrate the commitment to establishing servant leadership culture as Ron describes in 4th Dimension the process should be supported and facilitated from the top. If not the top administrator, someone very close to her level of authority and influence.

Resist the temptation to create a buffer layer between the leaders and the rest of the organization by inserting a third party. Do you know what it means when the leader of an organization says people may not provide honest feedback if they are the face of the effort to gather observations on internal culture? It means they already know that people don't trust them and that the culture isn't one of servant leadership.

Fair warning: This alone may be the most challenging section of this book and the most telling. In most organizations, wide opinions often exist when you attempt to reach consensus on how you want your own team to perceive your organization versus how they really do.

Pay attention - the depth of dissention on this question often correlates directly to the need for an intervention described in the second half of this book.

Let that sink in.

In other words, if this cultural transformation has a chance - this part should be hard.

Real = Hard.

Servant leaders do it anyway.

EXERCISE 3:
WHAT IS YOUR DESIRED INTERNAL BRAND?

Let's go back again to the idea that a brand creates an identity for your product or service. Or in this case an identity for your organization, your realm of public service. This identity is created by establishing some key characteristics and attributes those who work for your identify with your organization.

STEP 1: YOUR CORE TEAM

The good news is that if you followed the process in Exercises 1 & 2, you already have a representative core team built and familiar with the process.

The other good news is that by going through the process once already, you know who your stars are on that core team. And you know if there are members of that core team you may need to add or replace.

STEP 2: THE LIST

Your core team is going to repeat the process of establishing a list of crisp, meaningful characteristics or attributes you want your employees to associate with your organization.

Just like you did with the external exercise, you want at least three and no more than 7 desired characteristics or attributes.

There is no one set of characteristics that describe all organizations. The attributes you choose should be as unique to your organization as possible.

Some things to consider:

What types of positions and what types of employees will your organization most need to recruit and retain in coming years?

Are there key characteristics you know you need to display in order to complete major projects or successfully attain the goals of your organization?

Now - what are the attributes and descriptors that best describe the way your organization needs to be perceived in order to attract and keep the types of employees you need the most?

Who is your typical employee?

What is your employee turnover ratio?

Are your employees upwardly mobile or stagnant in your organization?

Have there been significant events or challenges in recent years that have positively or negatively impacted morale?

Remember that this effort is about servant leadership. Be sure to include some characteristics accordingly.

Again, expect this task to take some time. Anticipate the need for multiple constructive conversations. No two people come to work with the same motivations or needs. Thus establishing a list of desired internal brand identity will require all members of your core team to put aside the personal to create a shared aspirational description.

Once you have this accomplished you are ready to move on to the next step to determine your current brand.

EXERCISE 4:
DETERMINING YOUR CURRENT BRAND

Now that you know how you hope your employees perceive your organization, let's find out what they actually think of you.

This is your brand – even if it isn't one you are thrilled to own.

For many managers, this is where the process derails. The fear of less than glowing responses outweigh the desire for understanding. The chorus of naysayers convince the well intentioned leaders that the feedback will be negative, that hurdles to change perceptions are insurmountable and that the entire process will do more harm than good.

Here's the thing. If your employees think something less than flattering about your organization, are you better off being aware of those perceptions or would you rather continue to pretend they don't exist? Worse, can you continue to pretend they don't exist and suffer the symptoms?

This is the most important time to remember that you desire to be a servant leader. That means allowing all voices to be heard so that you can, in fact, serve the true needs of your organization. Serve your people.

I would again recommend using survey methodology to determine your internal brand. It is absolutely critical that anonymity is guaranteed and completely enforced.

STEP 1: THE SURVEY

Your internal survey could take one of two approaches or be a hybrid.

Option 1 is to simply send an open ended question: Please list the 5 characteristics or attributes you most closely associate with (organization).

Option 2 is to work with your core team to generate a list of possible characteristics and attributes from which the survey respondents will choose.

Include in your internal survey the crisp, meaningful attributes your core team agreed upon as your desired internal brand.

And take whatever vitamins you need to develop a thick skin because you must also include some characteristics that are less than desired. If you know there are some unfavorable connotations out there, or could be, same rule as last time. Don't bury your head in the sand. Put them on the list.

Here are some ideas:

Empathetic

Integrity

Exploitative

High
Performance

Dedicated

Cutting Edge

Caring

Confusing

Declining

Responsible

Difficult

Innovation

Dishonest

Accessible

Honesty

Service-oriented

Ineffective

Strong Work
Ethic

Lazy

Exhausting

Unreliable

Wasteful

Transparent

Values People

Resourceful

Trustworthy

Approachable

Friendly

High Quality

Inconsistent

Rude

Reliable

Acceptable

Forward thinking

Fun

Invests in
Improvement

Thriving

Warm

Good Stewards

Covert

Negative

Accountable

Option 3: Provide the list of potential characteristics and attributes, but also include an open ended opportunity for respondents to add their own.

The survey method for the internal brand analysis is typically less cumbersome than the external process. Create an online survey (do yourself a favor and select a platform that will automatically tabulate and graph results for you). Use your organization-wide email database to distribute the link to the survey. For those employees without access to email or daily work at a computer, provide an alternate method of anonymous pen & paper completion with a plan for manual entry online.

Though not encouraged, some organizations see better survey response when they offer some kind of incentive for completion. The problem with that is that it hampers the concept of anonymity and it sets a precedent that employees need a carrot to actively engage.

Regardless of your method, for the results to be valuable you must ensure that the respondents represent a large cross section of your organization. If you do not get equal participation from all functional areas and all levels of the organization, your results risk being skewed. In some manner keep track of responses by division or department. This is as easy as creating unique survey links by department. This information will be critical later.

Don't forget to do a calculation to determine how many returned surveys you need to make results valid.

STEP 2: THE RESULTS

As your internal survey period closes, tabulate the most frequent responses. This isn't the end all, be all definition of your internal perceptions of your organization, but it is a great start. This is particularly true if it is the first time you have conducted such an assessment and thus the results will serve as a baseline of understanding.

Now your team can move on to the next step.

INSIGHTS FROM RON

Stacy is so right about the way an organization's brand and its' culture are intertwined. We frequently use a process similar to what Stacy describes when a new senior executive comes on board to help the new leader determine whether the values plastered on the wall are actually being authentically lived out as that organization's behavioral norm (culture).

We consistently find that about 80% of employees cannot identify more than one or two of the organization's current stated values, even though they are typically posted all around the organization. And once they know what the stated values are, consistently about 80% of employees express a clear sense that the organization's behavioral norms are not aligned with those stated values.

One city manager that took her organization through a variation of this process deeply believed that her organization all knew the values and were all walking the talk. She was truly stunned when the assessment process revealed that such simply was not the case. In fact, her organization was very comparable to all others we had worked with... about 80% did not know the values, and once they knew what they were, about 80% did not give the organization very high marks for authentically walking the talk.

This particular organization took the wakeup call very seriously and spent a year going through a values definition and alignment process. Once they were armed with an awareness of the gap between what they said they wanted their culture to be and what their behavioral norms suggested it actually was, they took bold action to close the gap.

In other words... you do have a culture... you do have a brand reputation... but they may not be what you thought they were... and the only way to change your brand reputation is to close the gap between what you want your culture to be, and what your behavioral norms suggest it actually is.

Chapter Four:
The Road Map

Your team has worked diligently to facilitate two brand identity inventories - one external and one internal.

You are armed with the tabulated results.

Now what?

A word to the wise before you embark on this portion of the journey: **Cultural transformation is a lot like dieting**. You can make a bunch of extreme changes in a concentrated period of time and see dramatic results. Yet it is unlikely that you can sustain those dramatic changes over time and as a result you will likely see a regression to old ways. You are better off to take to process slow and make gradual changes that are well integrated in to day-to-day. This is the best way to ensure that the progress you make is permanent.

EXERCISE 5:
START & END POINTS

In this exercise, your team will map your desired brand and your actual current brand for both the external and internal focus areas. This process has a few organizational tricks that will matter later.

STEP 1: LIST THE DESIRED EXTERNAL BRAND

This step is clean and easy. List the 3-7 characteristics or attributes your core team established for your desired external brand on the far right hand side of the map.

Current	EXTERNAL BRAND ROAD MAP	**Desired**
		Accessible
		Reliable
		Resourceful
		Service Oriented
		Trustworthy

STEP 2: LIST THE ACTUAL EXTERNAL BRAND IDENTITY

Next, identify the 3-7 (whichever variable you used above) most commonly selected characteristics or attributes from your external brand survey.

Evaluate and list them on the far left hand side of the map, making sure to align in order any of these attributes that matched up with responses for desired brand.

List the characteristics that exactly match your desired attributes first.

List the characteristics that are positive though not exact matches to your desired attributes second.

List the characteristics that are less than flattering and/or definitely need to change last.

Current	EXTERNAL BRAND ROAD MAP	Desired
Accessible		Accessible
Friendly		Reliable
Good Stewards		Resourceful
Inconsistent		Service Oriented
Confusing		Trustworthy

STEP 3: ROADWORK

The Roadmap works from left to right.

Ideally, you have at least one characteristic match or near match. Draw a solid line for any exact matches. The road is in pretty good shape.

Likely, you have some near matches. For these, draw a dashed line. Think gravel road, passable but needs some smoothing over.

Also nearly certain, you have some places where there is no connection between your desired and actual descriptors.

Circle the characteristics that are unflattering and/or definitely need to change in your current brand. Assess the characteristics that are positive though not exact matches to determine the place they have in your desired list.

Star the characteristics on the right side that are not at all represented on the left side. These are the places where you will have to build the road.

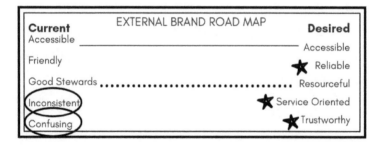

STEP 4: INTERNAL BRAND ROAD MAP

In this gathering, or at a separately scheduled one, repeat this process for your desired internal brand vs. your current internal brand.

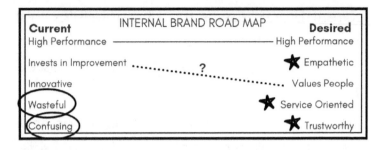

It is important to realize that you as the servant leader may need to carefully facilitate these constructive conversations. Some pathways will be clear. Others may not. There is likely to be much discussion about which attributes may or may not connect to each other.

I put a great example in the internal brand road map for you to consider. One of the desired characteristics is values people. One of the current characteristics is invests in improvement. Are these similar or not? I could argue this one both ways. What you need to do in a situation like this is go back to the original conversations about your desired internal brand that resulted in the list of characteristics. What was it about values people that was most important and distinctive?

There is no right answer and no decisions you make at this step in the process are set in stone. They are simply going to guide the future work of your team.

EXERCISE 6:
PLANNING YOUR ITINERARY

With your road maps complete, the next task for your core team will be to evaluate and complete a plan of action for your journey. The distance between where you want to be and where you just learned you really are will largely determine the approach.

If the pathway is a solid line, your work will involve understanding more about how your organization has effectively demonstrated and represented the aligned attributes.

Don't skip this analysis. It seems tedious, but it will provide insights on how and why some aspects of your culture are healthy. Look for patterns and cross tabulate responses to determine specific areas that are thriving and could be an example for the organization as a whole.

If the pathway is a dashed line, your work will involve transitioning perception from one similar attribute to another or reworking your desired attribute list to determine if the similar attribute is an acceptable substitute.

If there is no pathway, you really have work to do! And you really have an opportunity to serve your public and/or your organization to improve things. Ultimately, you want to remove the less than flattering attributes from association and replace them with the desired characteristics which are not yet captured.

The million dollar question is HOW?

For your external brand, most experts would now outline a multifaceted, all channels marketing strategy. This would require a significant investment of resources in to changing brand perception. Bright, shiny new wrapping paper as I like to say.

For your internal brand, many organizations would delve in to hiring a strategic leadership consultant to develop a comprehensive personnel overhaul or morale boosting perks. Another layer of bright shiny new wrapping paper.

How many times have you seen efforts like this? Another new campaign constructed outside your organization with no internal ownership. Especially in the public sector, these campaigns aren't worth the glitter it takes to wrap them.

Why?

This is the precise point where this book and this course of action related to branding differ from other publications and presentations on the topic.

For servant leaders, there is only one meaningful answer to the million dollar question.

For public serving organizations and for people serving leaders, your brand is about your team and it's about your culture.

Now, I will admit that your external brand can be bought. Throw enough resources at a campaign to promote the descriptors you want associated with your organization and in most instances you can achieve it.

However, it cannot be sustained over time without your people and your culture to back it up.

Your internal brand and as a result your culture can only be created, not purchased.

Your brand is your people. Period.

Your people and the way they serve. The way they build community. The way they lead.

This is the precise reason that for authentic servant leaders, brand and culture are intrinsically interwoven.

If you carry with you nothing else from this book - please, let this part sink in.

INSIGHTS FROM RON

Sometimes the most profound things are the most simple.

When you look at the 12 characteristics of authentic servant leaders identified in the writings of Robert Greenleaf, half of them are all about healthy relationships. At its' most basic level, culture is really all about how your people interact with each other and others.

In other words, culture is an organizational lifestyle that shapes interactions between people. And in the public sector your external brand is predominately shaped by the encounters that stakeholders have with your people. Those encounters are largely shaped by the authentic culture demonstrated in your organizational lifestyle.

When I was city manager in Garland, Texas, a private waste hauling company launched an incredibly aggressive campaign to get the city council to outsource all our solid waste collection under conditions that in my judgment were not in the public interest. They were making campaign contributions, hired lobbyists (including a former Mayor) as well as a PR firm to create media pressure, and sent out people on the speaking circuit to every civic club or organization that would have them.

I am an advocate of always considering all service options including privatization of services but let's just say that their presentations were designed more for political pressure than for thoughtful fiscal analysis!

Anxiety levels among our employees were very high. I began periodically meeting with our solid waste crews before they started their day, basically encouraging them that the way to save their jobs was very simple... they had to walk the talk of customer service that was beyond what anyone expected. We had previously launched an initiative to create a culture that was intensely focused on exceptional customer service, so my message was consistent with what they had been hearing... but now they faced a critical choice, would they become demoralized by the political attacks, or would they rise to the occasion and fight fire with exceptional customer service?

In other words, I told them that the way to defend themselves against the hostile takeover was not political... it was by walking the talk of our stated customer service values so passionately that citizens couldn't miss it and would not want to risk losing that exceptional service.

I emphasized to them that a typical citizen has a meaningful interaction with City Hall about once every two years. This means that every single interaction is an "aha" moment which will shape the perceptions of that citizen for a two-year period! As a result, every single interaction is a "super bowl moment" in which the goal should be to "wow" every stakeholder who interacts with them.

I knew from the meetings that our team was receptive to the message, but I knew we had won the war with a single phone call I got one day from a citizen. A random citizen was driving to work one morning and saw something that she was so stunned by that she just had to call the City Manager and tell him about it.

Sitting at a stop light on her morning commute she watched as a solid waste driver pulled his truck over into a parking lot, got out of the truck, and walked across a four-lane divided thoroughfare and picked up a bunch of newspapers that had blown against a fence. She had never witnessed such commitment to making a difference before and she was so stunned she just had to call and tell me about it.

The city's brand was dramatically shaped in an unbelievable way for the coming two years in the mind of that citizen based on a single encounter with a solid waste driver who she witnessed walking the talk of our values.

Your values are what you aspire to. Your culture is the living embodiment of what your authentic values actually are as reflected in your organizational lifestyle (whether they are the ones on the wall or not). And your brand is how your organizational lifestyle exhibits itself in interactions with your stakeholders.

The road map concept Stacy proposes is the path that connects these.

Part Two:
Creating Culture

Chapter Five:
The Role of Engagement

Civic Engagement

Customer Engagement

Employee Engagement

The term engagement is all the rage. Prime spot if you're playing buzzword bingo.

In the last several years countless books, workshops and blog posts acclaimed the virtues of engagement. Likewise, digital platforms and survey tools to measure and implement engagement abound. Engagement experts dot nearly every conference schedule.

For the most part, the engagement focus is external.

Here's the thing most organizations are missing – you can't do external engagement well if you aren't already knocking it out of the park on your internal engagement.

Uh-oh. That's right.

Engage your customers and your community all you want. But if you haven't first put forth the effort to engage internally, you haven't created the systems for the culture necessary to turn the results of the external engagements in to meaningful and sustainable wins for your organization.

So let's talk about the rules of internal engagement.

Rule 1: Make it intentional

Rule 2: Make it authentic

Rule 3: Make it a priority and follow through

Following these rules requires you to think ahead. It also calls on you to dig in a little to make an honest assessment of the purpose of engagement efforts.

For your efforts to have the best chance at long term sustainability, adhering to these rules is essential.

Keeping the rules in mind, let's cover a quick overview on the theory of engagement.

In my opinion, the best foundation for understanding the concept of intentional engagement is the International Association for Public Participation (iap2).

Their well-researched approach defines a spectrum for public participation that applies just as effectively to internal engagement.

iap2 is essentially a continuum that outlines the degree to which the audience is truly involved and authentically engaged.

Disclaimer:

The following is a summary of my understanding based on attending several iap2 workshops. I am not an iap2 trainer and I highly encourage you to research their work and attend official iap2 training sessions to learn more. (iap2.org)

According to iap2, the spectrum of engagement has five distinct levels of engagement. Each has its own intention for engagement to influence outcome.

Inform:

> Provide the audience with balanced and objective information to assist them in understanding the problem, alternatives, opportunities or solutions.

> To me, this is education. The one-way push of information with little intent to engage and little interest in two-way conversation.

Consult:

> To obtain audience feedback on analysis, alternatives and/or decisions.

> Inform and then ask for their feedback. In some way incorporate feedback in to analysis.

Involve:

> Work directly with the audience throughout the process so that their concerns and aspirations are consistently understood and considered.

> Concerns and aspirations then shape formulation of understanding of the problem, alternatives, opportunities and solutions.

Collaboration:

> Partner with the audience in each aspect of the decision including the development of alternatives and identification of the preferred solution.

Here there is a clear shift to sharing the power of decision making.

Empower:

Place the final decision in the hands of your audience.

A major focus of iap2 is aligning the degree of engagement with the true intention to incorporate input resulting from the engagement, not engaging for the sake of checking a buzzword box.

Engaging in a meaningful way with intention to allow the voices of the audience/ community to guide the end result.

If you aren't truly and honestly willing to do this – just stop now. Proceeding with any engagement effort under false premise does more harm than good, both externally and internally.

Authenticity is at the core of engagement and ultimately at the core of servant leadership.

Now, keep the concept of the continuum of engagement in mind as you consider your internal engagement efforts. For that matter, as you consider your efforts to infuse servant leadership into your culture. Engaging internally with your team is important, and doing so intentionally and authentically is critical.

Some things to remember:

The levels of engagement are not sequential, nor are they pre-requisites for each other.

There is no wrong method of engagement, so long as your efforts are intentional and authentic.

To be effective, you must clearly understand your own leadership style and your willingness to truly surrender control of the outcome.

Understand the capacity of your team and be realistic about the resources at your disposal when you seek to identify the best engagement method for each step of internal engagement.

Now let's translate the fundamentals of engagement to how they impact your effort to create an authentic servant leader culture.

Inform:

Certainly, simply informing your internal team is not going to win you any engagement innovation awards. But let's be honest, for most organizations keeping your internal team informed would be a major victory. This is particularly true when the challenge is communicating regularly about an intangible effort, versus the relative ease of providing updates on a construction or technology implementation project.

Still, if we consider engagement as a continuum let's remember that if we aren't covering the minimum level of engagement by consistently, effectively informing our team, we can't possibly focus on any other part of the engagement process. So let's start there.

An example of applying the "inform" approach to an internal engagement might be your intentional commitment to explaining the foundations of servant leadership and why it matters to you on a regular basis to your team. Maybe this takes the form of a section in your normal internal email update. Maybe you opt to create short videos to distribute digitally. Maybe you make it a topic for in person staff meetings or more informal team building events within your organization.

At least one of you will mutter to yourself at this point realizing that your organization does none of these things. Don't cancel the road trip. Just add these ideas as part of the journey.

Consult:

At the next level of the continuum you would engage your team to gain feedback on your intent to transform your culture into one focused on servant leadership. In doing so, it will be critical that you very clearly and honestly communicate that their feedback is valuable to you because you want to understand their perceptions, not because you can guarantee that their feedback will change the outcome. You are consulting them, not involving them.

This may sound harsh. In a way it is, but authenticity isn't always hearts and rainbows. By being clear from the beginning that your intent is to understand, you put to rest any misconceptions that feedback will influence your next steps. This alone can prevent the entire effort from derailing later due to an uprising that you didn't listen to advice provided.

Now, with that said, it seems to me it would be pretty unusual for someone who is truly a servant leader to take this approach. It is in many ways contrary to the core of servant leadership overall. Yet it may be the appropriate internal engagement method for certain stages of the process.

Involve:

This next level of engagement certainly is the first that feels intrinsically in line with the fundamentals of servant leadership. It is also the first that feels relevant to the way most of us conceive the purpose of engagement. At this level you not only intentionally involve members of your team to collect their feedback, but you incorporate that feedback in to the formulation of how the effort evolves.

An actual internal engagement scenario at this level may play out like this:

You present your plans to emphasize servant leader culture to your high level management team and seek their feedback on the plans. You then return to your office or to your small leadership team and incorporate their feedback. The key distinction is that their feedback at this engagement level has the ability to influence your plans. Of course, as with other levels of engagement, the critical component often overlooked is clearly communicating that you are seeking feedback and that feedback will be taken into account as plans are finalized.

Collaboration:

A truly collaborative approach is the pinnacle of internal engagement. If you hold true to this level of engagement it is also the first approach where you surrender control of the final outcome. Starting at the very beginning, you ask your top level managers to learn more about servant leadership. With a base understanding you then facilitate a conversation about the potential to shift to servant leadership culture in your organization. You do so entirely either confident that they will go along with the plan or willing to dismiss the effort if they are not in support of pursuing the transformation. You orchestrate a planning session to determine how the effort will roll out in your organization and the group process leads to consensus on an action plan that all will support.

Empower:

It goes without saying that a cultural transformation which results from this level of internal engagement has the best chances of success. Why? Ownership of the process.

Here's an interesting twist. What if in this stage you didn't collaborate with the same top level managers who are always part of shaping city projects? What if instead you went an extra step to ask each of them to appoint a representative from their departments? This requires an even greater surrender of control, but yields a deeper sense of ownership within the organization.

Remember this idea for later. In coming chapters you will be prompted to explore cultivation of brand ambassadors and culture champions for your organization. The intentional, authentic approach to internal engagement is critical to success in these efforts.

As you read the second half of this book keep all these levels of internal engagement in the back of your mind. Carefully consider which method of engagement best suits your efforts to spark cultural transformation. Also be mindful of the approach that best conveys your example of authentic servant leadership. Most importantly, whichever you choose - follow through.

The fastest way to kill an initiative is to starve it. Starve it of your time, your persistence and your attention.

This happens often quite unintentionally. The day to day responsibilities don't go away in lieu of your efforts to create a servant leadership culture in your organization. Schedules get overwhelmed. Meetings get canceled. Implementations get delayed. Seemingly more pressing matters emerge. And just like that you have signaled that other things are the priority. And gradually, the entire idea fades away.

The consequence reaches beyond just the demise of the cultural transformation. You have also demonstrated to your team that improving culture is not important. And in essence, they aren't important.

Your investment in the culture and environment where your teams spend more waking hours than they do at home with their families is your most valuable contribution as a servant leader.

Your lack of attention to culture translates in to a lack of ability as a leader.

Disturbance in cultural force will manifest over time, come what may. It will reveal itself in high turnover rates, in absence of strong recruiting pools, in reduced productivity, in apathy toward employee recognition programs and in decreased participation for once popular employee events.

Certainly you could choose to believe your existing culture is a healthy one.

Maybe it is. But how do you know?

INSIGHTS FROM RON

Stacy's focus on how the process unfolds influences the sustainability of the culture shift is precisely on target. As I mentioned above, when I was City Manager in Garland, we initiated a dramatic culture shift to create an aggressively action-oriented customer centric environment that empowered all employees to truly own solving problems. My role was to cast down the gauntlet that we wanted to create a customer centric culture beyond anything they had ever thought about before -- and to make it safe to think outside the box with a passionate commitment to making the vision become a reality.

Once I threw down that challenge (and they believed I was truly committed and would make it safe to do so)... the organization began to enthusiastically figure out how to close the very large gap between where we were and where we wanted to be. Initially our parks department came back with a highly innovative circular organizational chart. Everyone actually had two reporting hierarchies... a traditional operational structure, and a geographic neighborhood centric structure that crossed all traditional organizational lines. In other words, it was a customer centric organizational chart not organization centric – and it was developed by departmental employees not by the city manager.

Next, just as Stacy is recommending, we appointed an implementation team with no one higher than a mid-level manager on the team because they were the ones who best understood the work, and how to overcome the obstacles to great customer service. The implementation team ultimately developed an incredible plan for transforming the organization.

Just as with the phone call from a citizen regarding solid waste, I knew we had "made it" in the Police Department when I got a phone call one day from a citizen who was so stunned at what she had seen that she felt the need to call and tell the city manager about it.

Part of our culture shift had focused on creating a sense of ownership in geographic areas. In other words, it did not matter if you were police, fire, solid waste, parks, or anything else, you had traditional task-based job responsibilities, but more importantly, you had an overarching mission based job responsibility. The mission-based job responsibility was to take ownership in a designated neighborhood service delivery area, and work as a team across organizational lines to care for the assigned neighborhoods in every respect.

I will never forget the phone call I got from a mom in one of those neighborhoods. She lived across from a school crossing and mid-morning a dog had been run over in the intersection of the crossing where her kids walked to and from school every day. As this mom watched from her kitchen window, she saw something that was so stunning she just had to call the city manager and tell him about it.

As she stood at her kitchen window wondering what to do about the dog laying in the intersection she sees a police officer (who had ownership in this neighborhood) pull up at the intersection. He sees the dog lying in the street. She watches as he turns on his lights to block vehicles. She sees him get on his radio and then after he gets off of his radio, she is transfixed at her kitchen window as he gets out of his car and goes to the trunk and puts on a pair of nitrile gloves. Then this uniformed officer walks over and picks up the dead animal and moves him to the shoulder so he will not be hit again. Then he removes the gloves and places them in a bag in his trunk and returns to his vehicle. He continues to sit there until shortly an Animal Services vehicle shows up and removes the animal, after which the officer drives away.

That police officer did not focus on the tasks of this job... but on the mission. He saw himself as the guardian of that neighborhood and he knew that a dog run over in the intersection would negatively impact young children coming home from school that day. He didn't look at it and say "that's not my job". Instead, he looked at the situation and said "it is my mission to care for this neighborhood and the people who live here." He took his mission personally!

But make no mistake... that kind of commitment was a direct product of the engagement of the employees in building their own future with an organizational culture that they were proud of. The leader can demand compliance but commitment must be inspired. Compliance sustains only as long as "the boss is watching".

By contrast, because commitment depends on engagement of the heart instead of oversight of the hands, it becomes self-sustaining even absent direct oversight. Commitment comes when a leader casts a vision that employees can buy into, makes it safe for them to be passionately committed to making it a reality, and then engages them in a way that inspires them to go for it!

Chapter Six:
Which Comes First?

Which comes first - branding or culture?

It's a new version of a question without an answer. Because it isn't an either/or. The only answer is both.

If your roadmap reveals a divide between your desired and actual internal brand, point to culture.

If your efforts to cultivate a servant leader culture stall, point to branding.

If you don't have the right people, or people with the right priorities, you can't have a thriving servant leader culture.

If you don't have the right brand, both externally and internally, you won't get the right people or people with the right purpose to sustain your culture.

Branding and culture, particularly for public serving organizations and people serving leaders, are interdependent.

Here are two contrasting examples (fictional, though based on actual organizations) to illustrate this point.

Golden City is middle to upper middle class community with great schools. Successful at attracting new businesses and retaining satisfied residents, thus their tax base and resources are plentiful. The city is award winning and often cited as an example other cities aspire to.

Why can't we be more like Golden City? In Golden City they...

Yet strip back the glittery wrapping paper and what you might find is a team who describes the internal culture as greatly varying from the shiny exterior image.

- Pervasive lack of accountability
- Destructive interpersonal dynamics
- Noticeable waste of resources

- Disregard for internal expertise in favor of high priced consultants
- Challenge of thought is hushed
- Focus on the projects to win recognition rather than the people who make them happen.

Some refer to it as the city of golden handcuffs. They would leave in an instant, except the job pays so well they can't justify going somewhere else. Often outsiders can see that the organization is oriented toward a person or a group of elected officials. The entire organization is aligned to serve their egos, not the public.

Certainly Golden City still attracts highly skilled, experienced professionals. Those motivated by the exceptional compensation and opportunity to work on well-funded projects. Unfortunately their optimism and energy often fade once they are on the inside and see behind the curtain. As one of my mentors describes it, they gradually become like once ripe tomatoes rotting on a vine. Eventually word gets out in the professional community. If you can tolerate a soul sucking culture in exchange for handsome paychecks, Golden City is the place for you. If you are a passionate, energetic and creative talent - those in the know, including current Golden City employees, encourage you not to fall in to the golden handcuff trap.

Contrast this with Grit City.

Grit City is clinging to middle class identity. Recent shifts in economy and residential development further out of town have hit Grit City hard. Schools are still good, but test scores have shifted with the transitioning demographics of the community. The tax base just isn't what it used to be. As a result, elected officials and city administrators have scaled back on projects and personnel in recent years. They focus now on working smarter, on innovation and on partnerships.

While there isn't much sparkle on Grit City's exterior, inside the organization truly shines. An unintentional impact of the staff reductions was that more team members learned to do more than their original responsibilities. They had a chance to grow professionally. A strategic process was conducted, with significant, intentional internal engagement to determine the best ways to maintain services within resource limitations. Stakeholder's opinions and expertise was valued and they owned the result.

Because Grit City can't afford to hire fancy consultants for every project or strategic plan, employees gain experience facilitating these initiatives. While Grit City struggles to hold on to positions and couldn't even offer cost of living increases, they reward employees with other benefits like flex time, casual days and plenty of events where they gathered informally. Employees brought forward ideas for improvements and cost savings which were implemented and celebrated. They believe they have both the trust and influence to impact positive change in their organization.

When Grit City does have a position open they enjoy a diverse and impressive candidate pool. They have positioned themselves as a place that is rewarding both personally and professionally. The lack of big paycheck is made up for in the ability to work with bright, dedicated colleagues. The organization has a reputation of investing in their employees. None of this is so because it is printed in a glossy, slick recruitment ad. It happens because the word on the street, from people who work for and with Grit City, is that it is the place to be. Working for Grit City will make you a utility player and a leader.

If Golden City ever opened their eyes, took a deep breath and decided to take on their crisis, they'd have to admit that their internal organization can no longer hang on the coattails of their shiny external brand. Both their internal brand and their internal culture are a disaster.

Meanwhile Grit City's internal brand and internal culture are thriving. Though the community at large may have serious challenges, the internal organization is rising to meet them.

Obviously these are exaggerated versions of real organizations and I'm sure they sound familiar. But the point is critical.

Can you identify the key difference between Golden City & Grit City?

Golden City is focused on end product of projects and awards. Having the biggest, newest, fanciest trophies to satisfy ego.

Grit City is focused on people. On cultivating a can-do, nothing can keep us down spirit of innovation and enthusiasm.

In authentic servant leader organizations, healthy branding and culture come down to one simple question:

What are you making?

What are you, as a supervisor or manager, making?

At the end of the day, or end of the fiscal year, or end of the project plan you deem yourself successful how?

If the answer has anything to do with bottom line or completion date - you are wrong and yours is not a servant leader culture.

Your product is your people. Your success, or your failure, is your people.

Your brand is your people.

Your culture is your people.

The success of your organization is not up to you.

It is up to your people.

INSIGHTS FROM RON

Stacy is so right... your brand is your people... and your culture is your people.

That is why I like to refer to culture as an organizational lifestyle. The values you talk by writing them on the wall may be what your organization aspires to. But how those values are lived out in the hall every day is what your culture really is.

Behavioral norms ARE your authentic culture. And those behavioral norms are what determine your real brand (not just what you say it is).

For the desired values to permeate the organization, they must be consistently modeled at the very top of the organization (and at every level throughout).

Before the desired value and behaviors will become normative, employees must believe that their boss, and their bosses boss, and so on all the way up the ladder, are truly bought in and are role modeling the values that are hanging on the wall. Unfortunately, that is too rare in organizations.

SGR trains up to 1,000 local government employees per month and our most frequent class offering is Now That I am a Supervisor. For many years now, the number one question asked in the class has been "Why doesn't someone make my boss take this class?"

In other words, organizations are spending money to train their employees to try and establish certain behavioral norms, but then they fail to establish consistent systems to reinforce those norms and hold people accountable for walking the talk. The net result is not only wasted resources, but when employees see a gap between what the organization says its' values are, and what their behavioral norms demonstrate that the values really are, it creates a downward spiral in employee engagement, employee morale, and performance.

Jack Welch, the legendary CEO of GE famously said "culture eats strategy for breakfast." In other words... it all comes down to your people. If you are not investing in them, impressing upon them the values that matter, and inspiring them to be their best selves, you are failing as a leader.

Chapter Seven: Crafting your Culture Story

By now hopefully you are nodding a little bit. Maybe making notes in the margins. And almost certainly you are tired of waiting to hear exactly HOW to shift your internal brand and culture.

So let's dive in.

We are going to spend the rest of the book working on your internal brand and culture. The reason is simple: You have to get your house in order first. If you can successfully transform your internal culture to one that reflects authentic servant leadership, that shift will inherently result in creating the external brand you desire.

Keep in mind as you work through the remainder of the exercises in the book that you should be aligning your efforts to create a servant leader culture, which will create an internal brand, which will result in an external brand.

EXERCISE SEVEN:
TRACING THE ROUTES

Assemble your core team. Go back to your roadmap. Find the attributes circled and starred. If you are a lucky bunch with no circles or stars, look at your dotted lines.

Facilitate a brave, honest session with your core team. This can be structured in the time format that works best for your team. This is heavy stuff and can often stoke some strong emotions. Not only may your team need time to release steam, your ability to hold true to the ground rules yourself may require stepping away.

Some organizations may be able to complete Steps 1-3 in one gathering. Others may have to bail midway through Step 1. Either one is fine.

Do what is best for your team.

There are some ground rules to keep in mind as you proceed in this process.

Ground Rule 1: Restrain yourself from getting defensive or from justifying circumstances that may have led to negative attributes. Circling around the past at this point does only one thing - gets you nowhere.

Ground Rule 2: Changing your internal brand and culture takes more than changing your org structure or policies. These may indeed be part of the solution, but just as people are the root of success, people are the root of the solution. If you stop short of a full effort to inspire your people to embody your desired brand, you are doing a half donkey job.

With these ground rules in place, ask the hard questions.

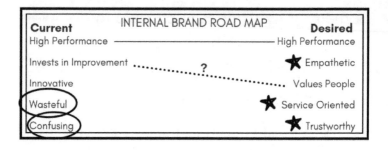

STEP 1:

WHY DO THE NEGATIVE, CIRCLED ATTRIBUTES RESONATE?

Because you have taken the care to assemble the right core team and you have created an atmosphere without penalty for vulnerability, you will learn much just by asking this question.

Take notes. For this first portion of the session, stay focused on the why.

If the group starts to stray in to solutions, promptly bring them back to the why.

Group the responses by similarity or root cause.

Stop short of working on solutions just yet.

STEP 2:

WHY DON'T THE STARRED ATTRIBUTES RESONATE?

Same open, authentic conversation. Focus on the why, not the solution. Take notes. Group the responses by similarity or root cause.

STEP 3:

COMPARE THE RESULTS FROM STEP 1 & STEP 2.

I'll bet you Skyline Chili* that there will be responses from both that share a common theme. Group them.

> *if you don't know what Skyline Chili is, come see me in Ohio. You're missing out.

It is possible, though less likely, that no root causes are shared. That means you have multiple, independent fires burning. Not impossible to fight, but you will have to carefully plan your attack.

You may have leaders who aren't leading at all.

You may have a culture where mediocrity is the norm.

You may have systems and processes that are fossils from another time.

Moving forward in this cultural transformation will require you and your core team to act as what I call Organizational Anthropologists.

You need to dig through some old, dusty stuff and figure out how to rework your organizational structure and your day to day processes to align with the new reality you are trying to create.

Another reason it is so critical to have both the leadership and fortitude of the person at the top of the organization as well as the whole-hearted buy-in of those from all levels of the organization who will have to be on this dirty, sometimes treacherous journey together.

This may be a great opportunity to encourage your core team to read or re-read Ron's 4th Dimension Leadership book. In all likelihood, some of the common struggles he identifies in the book are at play in your organization.

The stuff you excavate in this part of the process is a treasure and will become the foundation of your efforts.

EXERCISE EIGHT:
CULTURE CREED

The goal of this exercise will be to draft a culture creed.

A proclamation of what the internal culture of your organization stands for and what the collective whole will not accept.

List the root causes for each cluster of your results from Exercise Seven.

Assemble your core team. Same ground rules apply.

Ground Rule 1: Restrain yourself from getting defensive or from justifying circumstances that may have led to negative attributes.

Ground Rule 2: Changing your internal brand and culture takes more than changing your org structure or policies. These may indeed be part of the solution, but just as people are the root of success, people are the root of the solution. If you stop short of a full effort to inspire your people to embody your desired brand, you will fail.

This approach is crafted to keep your team away from policy or structural solutions. In a very free, brainstorming manner ask your team for feedback to the following:

COMMON THEME A

STEP 1: To address this common theme, what things should our organization expect, demand and hold each other accountable to demonstrate?

All responses should be formatted using a collective pronoun "we" followed by an affirmative verb.

i.e. – we expect accountability, not we don't accept mediocrity

STEP 2: To address this root cause, what things does our organization need to refuse to accept?

Again, all responses should be formatted using a collective pronoun "we" followed by a verb. Very skilled teams can phrase these using an affirmative verb without a negative. This is something to aspire to, but it is challenging and can stifle the process for most teams. Instead, format as necessary. If you desire, go back at the end of this step and attempt to rephrase removing the negative clause without changing the intent of the statement.

i.e. – we know that accountability to each other and to the public is essential to our collective strength

STEP 3: Repeat Steps 1 & 2 for each root cause cluster.

STEP 4: Refine. Are there any duplicates? Any items that can be combined? Any similarities that may allow you to group sentiments? Your goal in this step is to refine your proclamations in to a concise, meaningful culture creed.

Ask yourselves: When we distribute this organization wide, will it be clear what we are trying to do?

Will employees be able to identify with the culture creed?

INSIGHTS FROM RON

Stacy has mapped out a very clear and easy to follow strategy for starting to craft your culture story. The path is easy, but the journey is difficult.

The journey to success requires a deeply committed hunger to know the brutal truth and the emotional intelligence to handle the truth. Too many leaders go to great lengths to avoid hearing anything that conflicts with their idealized view of what they think reality is.

One organization I worked with had a leader who lived in denial. He thought morale was good. He thought people saw him as the leader. He thought people supported him. But nothing could be further from the truth.

His executive team conveyed to him some significant concerns among employees and at their strong urging he agreed to have a committee prepare and conduct an employee survey to develop a better understanding of the issues, and then presumably be able to act upon those concerns and issues. Each of the executive team members appointed three employees who were opinion leaders in their areas to serve on the committee to facilitate the survey process.

The committee did its' work admirably and conducted the surveys and follow up conversations with employees. The original intent was that their report was to be presented back to the executive team for consideration and action. But because this leader was not an authentic servant leader, he circumvented the process to avoid being faced with reality. He went to each committee member personally and asked them if there were any major issues about his performance that he needed to know about.

It is not hard to predict what happened in those one on one meetings. The top executive in an organization goes directly to the office of front and mid-level employees and surprises them with the question "is there anything I need to know about me?" Employees were intimidated by his presence and did not feel comfortable being brutally honest. As a result, they gave very generic answers that did not honestly convey the negative feedback about the culture that the executive had overtly created even though such was actually contained in the survey.

Then he went to the executive team and told them that he had already visited with each of the committee members and they had provided him with his version of "there is nothing to see here... move along."

In other words, all of the executive team members had heard from their employees that there were really significant issues amongst employees. A process was set up to achieve honest feedback, and then the leader circumvented the process to avoid being faced with the truth and making sure that there was no report presented that would conflict with his distorted view of reality.

His insecurity and lack of courage as an authentic servant leader to confront reality plunged the organization to even lower depths of morale and employee disengagement. Weak leaders think if they avoid letting the truth be documented, then the bad news doesn't exist.

But reality is just the opposite. Strong leaders who have the greatest credibility with their organizations are those who are brave enough to hear the truth, and emotionally intelligent enough to respond the truth with constructive, action-oriented improvements.

Stacy has mapped out a process to pursue greatness if only you are brave enough to follow it.

Chapter Eight:
Crucial Foundations

Before we get into a step by step guide for rolling out your servant leader culture transformation here are some overarching, ongoing crucial foundations for this process.

Voice

Realize it or not, as you work through this process you are establishing your internal brand and culture voice. Doing so with intention and consistency is imperative.

What does this mean? How would you respond if I asked you to describe the persona of your brand and culture?

You will not be the only person responsible for championing your brand and culture. You won't be the only person to write or speak about things that impact brand and culture. You won't be there to train every staff person, to speak with every constituent or to conduct every performance evaluation.

The voice of your brand and culture must pervade your organization. For this to happen it must be crystal clear and widely reinforced.

So, what is your brand and culture voice?

Bring your core team together to create your culture character. Often this works by having small teams work to create a character first and then combine parts to make one that everyone agrees is representative of who you want to be and how you want to be perceived.

For example, here is the voice I use in my current organization:

- Over 50
- Well educated
- Calm and patient
- Conservative
- Risk Averse
- Humble
- Resourceful

- Grateful
- High standards
- Treasures integrity

So each time I write myself or on behalf of my elected officials or top administrators, I get into character and think like this persona.

In Grit City, the character might be:

- About 35 - 45
- Energetic
- Optimistic
- Hip
- A natural Coach
- Restless with a purpose
- Resourceful
- Confident
- Trendsetter
- Early   adopter

Disclaimer: Before anyone gets bent out of shape about these sweeping generalizations, particularly about age, discerning the unique characterization of your voice and your audience are a key part of marketing. You wouldn't write a commercial for a children's toy the same way you would write one for a retirement plan.

Voice matters because you are going to cultivate and attract what you present. Your brand voice tells those within and outside your organization who you are. Your culture brings this voice, and in turn your brand, to life.

Language

Creating a common language is central to any organizational change.

The reason it is imperative that your core team carefully craft your culture creed is that it will become the center of your common language.

The phrases you create as part of the culture creed will appear together and separately in every facet and function of your organization.

- Recruiting materials
- Training guides
- Performance evaluations

- Annual reports
- Employee awards

Communication

It is imperative that as you work through each of the exercises in this book you communicate beyond your core group to the entire organization.

A simple e-mail describing the results of each exercise and a summary of next steps is all you need.

This accomplishes several things:

First, it prevents the perception that any of this is happening behind a cloud of super-secrecy. If rumors start circling about a select few determining the destiny for the uninformed whole, your efforts will quickly hit a roadblock.

Second, it provides an opportunity for those not on the core team to understand process and to contribute feedback. Perhaps it is best in your organization to suggest feedback come directly to you, if necessary in anonymous format. Perhaps your organization is healthy enough that you can suggest relaying feedback to members of the core team for representation. If this doesn't place too much pressure on core team members, do it. If they tell you (which means you asked them!) that they are not comfortable with this, take the heat yourself.

Finally, it just may bring new core team members on board. If there are individuals who are consistently making valuable contributions following each communication update, consider adding them to the core team. If it is best in your organization to not appear to pick and choose new members, that is completely understandable. But keep these individuals in mind for an equally valuable role that will come later in the process.

Honesty

Some people need brutal honesty and minimal ambiguity to be comfortable with change. It is important to include some statements in all communication which acknowledge the degree of change necessary to accomplish the cultural transformation, the commitment to make those changes and the timeline for those to occur.

WIIFM?

To make the shift to a servant leader culture throughout your organization it will be necessary to answer this question.

What's in it for me?

What are the crucial elements that will lead to buy in?

The following may just be the secret recipe, particularly as we focus on servant leadership culture.

- Appeal to intrinsic motivation
- Opportunity to serve others or the common good

- Multi-factor benefits - personal & professional, satisfaction & growth

INSIGHTS FROM RON

Another way to describe finding your voice is having "emotional intelligence and self-awareness" at an organizational level. In other words, emotional intelligence and self-awareness at an individual level is the foundation for reaching your potential. But the same thing is true for an organization or a community as well.

This may best be illustrated in economic development terms. I worked with one city who hungered for a high-end hotel to locate there. They had a designated location, their master plan called for it, they had the zoning in place, and the council gave marching orders for the economic development staff to make securing a hotel a top priority. Unfortunately, they were openly critical of the Economic Development Director because she had failed for several years to achieve their goal of a hotel.

But here was the deal – the city had no highway frontage; no corporate campuses; no tourism venues; nothing at all that made it reasonable for a high-end hotel to consider locating there. The failure was not of the Economic Development Director. The failure was at an organization wide leadership level. There was such low degree of emotional intelligence and self-awareness on the part of the governing body, and thus of the organization, that their goal was unattainable no matter how much they wanted it to be. They simply did not understand their own community's attributes (or the drivers of hotel location decisions) to be able to succeed. Their lack of self-awareness means that they were trying to brand themselves in a way that was detached from reality.

Now do not misunderstand me. Your present state is not destiny. I have worked with multiple organizations who have done what no one thought could be done, and as a result changed their brand, their voice and their destiny. But in every successful case, they began the journey with clear-eyed self-awareness of their current brand and voice, then they defined what they wanted to be different in the future, they mapped out a realistic pathway for making the desired state a reality, and then they committed the necessary resources to make it a reality.

You will never control your future until you understand your present; and part of understanding your present is defining your voice.

Chapter Nine:
Brand Ambassadors and Culture Champions

For many years I enjoyed invitations to present conference sessions, host webinars and write articles about creating Brand Ambassadors in the public sector.

Traditionally, brand ambassadors are individuals who positively represent the brand. In the private sector these individuals are often paid and are known as spokespeople rather than brand ambassadors. Their value to the brand is based on their favorable reputation and the desire of others to follow their lead.

In recent years, there has been a significant shift in how companies are approaching brand representation. This is arguably a result of paid celebrity spokespeople falling from grace. It also steps from changes in consumer behavior which indicate that individuals are more likely to purchase/support a brand because someone they know and trust does.

Enter the role of "common man" brand ambassadors. Years ago I played the role as a member of a nationwide network of working moms who got coupons for consumer products and then wrote reviews on product sites. Now platforms like Amazon reviews and Yelp make the ability to gain and provide consumer feedback a part of everyday life.

What does this mean for the public sector?

I argue that public sector organizations have three audiences at the ready to serve as brand ambassadors. The first, and most valuable in my opinion, are your employees. The second are highly engaged members of your community who serve on boards, commissions or other leadership roles. The third is your community at large.

Exploring all three of these is a full conference presentation and a book of its own. Relevant to now is a description of how your employees can serve as brand ambassadors.

In the context of the 4th Dimension Leadership series, it is appropriate to refer to your employees not only as Brand Ambassadors, but ultimately as Culture Champions.

So.

How do you know who your Culture Champions are?

How do you develop new Culture Champions?

Identifying Culture Champions

Remember when I told you earlier about The Leadership Vortex? How there are just some members on any team who are always engaged, always in it for the right reasons and always willing to do what it takes?

And certain employees authentically represent the attributes that you most want identified with your brand. Certain employees embody the culture phrases in your culture creed.

They may not be the ones who step up all of the time to lead projects. They may not be outspoken. They probably don't have leadership titles. But they are leading by example. Day-in, and day-out.

Ask anyone in my organization to name our Culture Champions and I bet they would come up with the same ones I do.

- Our HR Manager who worked her way up through organization and knows everyone here, regardless of position, by name.
- Our front desk Receptionist who knows more about this city than anyone else and patiently answers every resident call with a smile like it is her first one of the day.
- Our Business Manager who showed us all how to stay devoted to service even as

he was facing a series of potentially devastating health crises.

- Our Police Captain who is a kind, soft spoken giant without a touch of authoritarian nature.
- Our Law Director, who is often berated, chronically overburdened with needed-it-yesterday requests yet I've never, ever heard him play the martyr.

And our greatest legend here, our ultimate Culture Champion, is our former City Manager. As the story goes, an elderly woman once called his office because of the condition of her driveway. She wasn't physically able to do the needed work, didn't have family in town and she couldn't afford to hire anyone. So he quietly slipped out. He went to get the supplies and sealed her blacktop in his suit pants and dress shoes on his lunch break. And he made every attempt to make sure no one ever knew what he had done. Still eventually the word of good deeds always gets around.

It is no coincidence btw that our culture persona sure resembles him and our organization seems to attract and celebrate those who follow his example! This includes his successor and my current boss who is a servant leader to the core.

EXERCISE NINE:
CULTURE CHAMPIONS

STEP 1: Gather your core team. Present to them the concept of Culture Champions. Have your culture creed on hand, maybe even up on the wall.

Who in our organization most embodies this?

Only rule is that they cannot name themselves!

Again- in a free, brainstorming manner work together to make a list. No dissension at this point. That will be facilitated later.

STEP 2: Reach a consensus on at least three Culture Champions for your organization. If you have a robust and very impressive list, select more. Ideally there is some diversity by department, tenure and demographics.

STEP 3: You will then divide the work among small core team groups to write a one page summary of WHY this person is a Culture Champion.

HOW do they demonstrate the culture phrases in the manifesto?

Here's the question I get often. Keep these selected individuals a secret or not? Depends on your organization. Depends on the circled attributes on your road map and your culture creed! Element of surprise is powerful. But so is authentic engagement.

In the end I always advise that you do whatever is most in line with the culture shift you hope to accomplish.

INSIGHTS FROM RON

In every community, there are individuals who derive their sense of personal worth and meaning by regularly appearing at city council meetings to blast everything the city does. They specialize in baseless allegations, conspiracy theories and negativity. In their world, every solution has a problem.

In one city I worked with, the mayor just knew that our most vocal critic would come around if only he were involved enough to understand what we were doing and why. Over much advice to the contrary she appointed him as a co-chair of the bond committee to develop a water bond program. Predictably, instead of his engagement bringing him around, it simply provided him a bigger platform and greater credibility for his baseless criticisms of the city and the bond program. And for the first time in memory, the city had a water bond program fail at the polls.

When you select leaders who are not truly committed to the mission and goals of the effort, failure is predictable. What is true in a political environment is also true within organizations as well.

One of the most common leadership mistakes is appointing committee members based on seniority, level of leadership or organizational politics rather than on what they bring to the table and their heart commitment to the task at hand. These leaders either make the mistake of under estimating how much it matters who serves on a committee, or that having the "aginners" on the committee will bring them around.

And just as with putting the city critic on the bond committee, placing an employee on a culture committee who is a purveyor of negativity, or who does not have a heart commitment to the mission, will make failure predictable.

It is important to understand that a culture is really an organizational lifestyle. It is the behavioral default

Chapter Ten:
Ready. Set. Launch.

Give your core team a chance to work through how they think the servant leadership culture transformation could roll out in your organization

As I have throughout this book, I am going to provide some guidance for how to do this. Unlike the rest of this book, it will not be step by step. It will be ideas, examples and guidance.

Why?

Because the journey from here is now in your hands and the hands of your core team. It has to be.

Efforts that are outlined and dictated by an outside force have no sustainable impact on culture.

Yes, even those orchestrated by the most experienced and renowned of leadership consultants. You and your organization must draw the roadmap and own the journey.

With that said, here are some components you may want to consider:

Present your culture creed.

I'd think about doing this in the form of a video. I'm always thinking about getting the most bang for the effort. A video allows all arms of the organization to hear the same information, now and in years to come. There's some serious shelf value here. It also opens up options for delivery.

Perhaps senior leadership or representatives from the core team travel from department meeting to department meeting, video in tow. Perhaps the premier is at an all-organization gathering. Perhaps it is sent electronically organization wide all at one time.

Post the video in the employee section of your website.

Provide links to the documents that summarize the work of your core team, including the culture creed.

This should go without saying, but make recognition of each of your core team members an important part of however your first share their work.

Spread the Word

Work with your internal communication team to get an inventory of all available internal communication networks. Determine how you include servant leadership culture messaging on a regular basis. Maybe this initiative warrants the creation of a stand-alone internal newsletter or e-newsletter.

My personal recommendation would be an e-newsletter with the ability to track open rate and click ratios. That way you can tell if the interest ever stalls over time and you can revive it with special features or exclusive content.

Celebrate your Culture Champions

Either as part of your initial video or in a closely following communication, it is time to celebrate the Culture Champions you identified.

Maybe you drive home the new servant leader culture transformation by highlighting one each day following the video premier. Include them and the descriptions created by your core team on your website, on your intranet, in your internal newsletters. Post them, physically and digitally, every place you can.

In the age of social media, I really love to see places that post publicly celebrating their Culture Champions. It is a clear statement that their example is valuable to your organization. These individuals serve your community every day and the community should be as proud of them as you are. Plus then their friends and family get the chance to congratulate them.

Make it Personal

Create a series of nice cards, almost like a playing deck. Put your logo or some other meaningful identifier on the front. On the back list each of the phrases from the culture creed and/or the desired internal brand attributes.

Produce a deck to give to each employee. This doesn't have to be fancy and expensive. They can be made out of business card templates on a black and white printer with just as much meaning.

Ask each employee to keep the deck on or in their desk.

At the start of each week, perhaps prompted by a weekly/monthly servant leader email (hint, hint), prompt each employee to pick the attribute or phrase that they commit to embody that week or month.

Supervisors can encourage employees to share in regular meetings which they selected and why.

Big Wall

Find a large wall in a common hallway or area in each facility where you have groups of employees working. If you don't have the physical space, make a virtual one. Maybe this is done at a special event or maybe during a special effort to focus on culture.

Give each employee a sticky note.

Ask them to pick from the following phrases and complete them.

- **Because working here gave/gives me the chance to...**
- **My WHY is...**
- **The coworker I most admire is...because.......**
- **It makes me the most proud to work here when.....**

Your team can surely think of even more appropriate phrases to include. Come up with enough and maybe the big wall rotates with a new prompt every so often throughout the year instead.

INSIGHTS FROM RON

As referenced earlier, when I was City Manager in Garland we launched an aggressive and dramatic culture shift towards a servant leadership and citizen centric value system that paid huge dividends in the quality of citizen service. One of the core strategies recommended by our employee led culture implementation committee was development of a culture video (just as suggested by Stacy).

In our case, the culture video was designed to be multifunctional. First it was used to communicate the new cultural values and organizational lifestyle to all current employees in a compelling way that everyone would understand and remember. And second it was used during all new employee orientations along with a workbook to help them understand what we really meant. But the same video was also designed from the beginning to be incorporated into our hiring and promotional processes.

Before any candidate (either internal or external) was hired, they had to view the video in advance of meeting with the interview panel who incorporated a discussion about the values we had embraced in the organization, what the individual thought about them, and how they saw themselves walking the talk of those values in their new role if they were selected.

In other words... we were not hiring a resume – we were hiring people, including the values that made them tick, and determining whether they would be a good fit for our unique environment was critical.

If you are going to create an authentic servant leadership culture, it is absolutely essential to create alignment between all of your systems including how you interview and promote. Developing a well-done culture video is one of several core strategies that will help you to define what authentic servant leadership looks like inside your organization, to communicate it clearly and persuasively, and then use it as a tool to do a better job of hiring and promoting people who are a fit with your desired culture.

Chapter Eleven:
Culture Vultures

It is a complete coincidence, but perhaps no coincidence at all, that Culture Vultures are the topic of Chapter Eleven. After all, Chapter Eleven is a term commonly associated with the threatened demise of an organization.

Many years ago, the term culture vulture was coined to describe an individual who devours any and all artistic and cultural offerings.

My connotation of the term is quite different.

Each time I work with an organization or present this topic in workshops, my description of Culture Vultures in organizations tends to be a crowd favorite.

Inevitably as you launch this servant leader culture transformation some Culture Vultures will emerge.

You know the ones. They are menacing. They pick at everything. Their mere presence instills fear of doom.

Culture Vultures spend time picking at efforts and pointing out why they won't work.

Culture Vultures rebuke efforts to incorporate culture into every day – to put people first. They are the first to block a people first approach with a legal risk and proclaim that policy, technology or marketing are the better areas to make the change.

Every organization has them. And unfortunately even the best efforts to transform culture won't destroy them all.

SO HERE ARE SOME WAYS TO DEAL WITH THEM.

Name them. As you conduct culture sessions, introduce everyone to the "Culture Vulture" persona just as I've described them here. Of course never use actual names or descriptions of people in your organization.

Don't feed them. Draw upon a basic tenant from Buddhist meditation. What you feed with your energy will grow. What you starve of your energy will die. Not only do this outwardly, but you must commit to not let the Culture Vultures take up residence eating up your insides either.

Don't hide from them. Create an expectation that we all own this culture and that none of us will feed the Culture Vulture.

Take a hint from the force. If we keep focusing on the things we hate, we will lose. The way we win is by saving the things we love.

I recently received an email from someone who attended a conference session where I presented the threat of Culture Vultures in your organization. She told me that she recounted the content to her coworkers, including a few who were pesky Culture Vultures. And days later one of her coworkers spoke up to the menacing Culture Vulture during a meeting and simply said, "Hey. Quit being a Culture Vulture."

This is a product of a common language and a common understanding. It is a clear demonstration of how naming Culture Vultures shifts energy toward those working for change and starves those who relentlessly strive to pick it apart.

Converting a Culture Vulture

With the right approach, it may be possible to convert a Culture Vulture.

One of the portions of Ron's 4th Dimension Leadership book that really struck me was the section on stealth incompetents. At the time I made a note about how organizations manage underperformers, how they contain potential damage caused by Culture Vultures.

What if we were bold enough to intervene instead of ignore? What if one-on-one, the known least-engaged employees were asked if they'd like a chance at finding a way they could find meaning and satisfaction instead of just a paycheck?

The intervention would involve some career counseling to determine whether personal competency, technical competency and/or professional competency are the root of the disengagement.

This may sound far-fetched and indeed in some cases it will yield little results.

But if you are truly a servant leader, you value your people, even the lowest common denominators.

If you are an authentic servant leader, you invest in your people even when they seem uninterested or uncommitted.

What you just may find is that they have been waiting for someone to notice. Their lack of engagement is really a cry for help. They are jaded and disenchanted because they perceived that no one noticed their detachment. Or if anyone did notice, they didn't care.

Take a deep breath and have the conversation.

INSIGHTS FROM RON

In an age of increasing disconnection from institutions of all sorts, how we manage our brand externally actually translates into how we manage relationships.

John Cleese famously described the main problem as "People who do not have a clue do not have a clue that they do not have a clue." Nowhere is this truer than when it comes to brand management. Organizations who have the absolutely worst brand reputation are often the ones who don't have a clue that they have a horrible reputation (nor of what they are actually doing to create the bad reputation).

A few years ago, I was recruiting a city manager for an organization that had a well-known reputation as a political meat grinder that had gone through multiple city managers in the last few years. When their top choice insisted on a stronger contract than normal to be willing to come, the governing body was offended and said "We do not want to hire anyone who does not understand what a phenomenal opportunity it is."

In other words, this particular city council did not have a clue and they did not have a clue that they did not have a clue about how bad their reputation was – nor did they have a clue that the bad reputation was largely created by THEM. Their disconnect with reality reinforced the very reasons that a great manager would insist on a better than normal contract.

Instead of hiring a great city manager who had the strength of character and professional skills to help that city council overcome their dysfunction and become a high performing organization, they opted for a candidate who would be compliant with their blind commitment to mediocrity.

Any time a leader seeks the bland comfort of employees who tell them what they want to hear instead of hungering for brutal honesty, they are leading the organization in a steady march towards mediocrity.

Leaders do the same thing when they allow the perspectives of culture vultures to be normalized. When leaders leave a vacuum, by not constantly talking about culture and expected organizational culture norms, the voices of negativity will always fill the void. They cook up wacky conspiracy theories, they convince people they are being victimized and just like real vultures they thrive on picking away every semblance of the organization's intended cultural identity until the organization begins to resemble a sun-bleached pile of dead men's bones.

Culture vultures thrive in an environment devoid of constant and effective communications about "the why" of it all. To overcome them, you as the leader must: create aligned operating systems that enforce and reward the values you aspire to make authentic; be passionately committed to walking the talk every single day so that people know YOU are authentically committed to them; and communicate constantly so that you fill every encounter you have with such passion for the values that there is no oxygen left in the room for those who want to tear down and destroy with their commitment to mediocrity.

Chapter Twelve:
Culture Transformations

As Ron described in 4th Dimension Leadership, imparting a sustainable servant leader culture requires the alignment of systems.

The first of which is your organizational culture. Now that we have covered how to make this happen, let's take just a short review of how successful organizations have incorporated culture into many of the other systems.

The best way to tackle the systems outlined in the rest of this chapter is to once again gather your core team.

Instead of them working together again, use this opportunity to spread their influence.

Each of them becomes a team captain. They adopt one of the organizational systems. They select their own team of promising contributors from throughout the organization. Their team reviews the system currently in place and then makes a recommendation for how to realign the system with the culture code.

Please recognize that this is a valuable opportunity for some promising leaders from your core team to gain experience building and managing a cross-departmental team.

Recruiting

What do your recruiting materials say about your organization? Are they in line with your desired external and internal brand? Do they include phrases from your culture creed?

Candidate Screening

What processes do you use for candidate screening? Are there forms or first interview questions that gather some sense of the candidate's fit with your desired culture? When candidates come in for an initial interview, who sits on the interview panel? Any culture champions there with the primary purpose of determining organizational fit?

Onboarding

How are your desired culture and the attributes of your desired internal brand incorporated into your onboarding process? Be honest, other than a meeting to do tax forms do you have an onboarding process? At a minimum - show them the video! A simple and meaningful way to infuse culture in to onboarding is to involve your core team and your Culture Champions. Maybe you host a quarterly gathering for all new employees where you introduce them - personally - to your Culture Champions. Maybe you take it a step further by asking Culture Champions to become assigned one-on-one organizational mentors for each new employee. What better way to impart culture?

Re-boarding

My absolute favorite question to ask during my conference presentations is how many organizations do re-boarding. Rarely does a hand go up, but when I describe what I mean by re-boarding nearly every head nods. Solid re-boarding efforts are few and far between, particularly in the public sector. Essentially this involves an intentional effort to bring employees back through a process after their initial entry into employment.

Maybe it is at regular intervals like every five years. In this scenario, it could involve a career trajectory assessment and opportunities for future leadership experience.

Performance Evaluations

Do your performance evaluations include assessment of desired internal brand attributes and phrases from your culture creed? This act alone conveys to your employees that the effort isn't just talk. That it will be measured and their contributions to culture will be evaluated. Take that Culture Vultures!

If an employee's embodiment of your desired culture is never measured and therefore is not important to their supervisor, then it isn't important to the organization and it isn't important to the employee.

Employee Recognition

This one should be easy to pull off. Tie your employee recognition program to your internal brand attributes and your culture creed.

Solicit nominations each year for Culture Champions.

Don't give this designation out unless individuals really deserve it.

Watering down standards will dilute the power of the designation and render the recognition program meaningless.

Find small, inexpensive ways to provide recognition as well. I hate cheesy trinkets like pins. But I still have a handwritten business card size note my former boss wrote to me thanking me for something I did that demonstrated our core values. Frequent and authentic goes a long way.

INSIGHTS FROM RON

Another way of describing a systems based approach to creating culture is very simply "predictable inputs create predictable outcomes."

Too many organizations have siloed systems for recruiting, selecting, onboarding, developing and evaluating leaders (and yes managing your brand) that have been designed independently from each other.

This lack of integrated systems not only sends mixed messages to the organization, it often actually advances conflicting value systems and priorities.

Systems must be carefully designed to holistically nurture, reinforce, enforce and hold everyone accountable for a coherent set of values on an integrated basis – or an organization will never create a consistent and authentic servant leadership culture.

Creating aligned systems is only part of the

formula for creating an authentic servant leadership culture but it is an essential part. Failure to do so will ensure failure.

Closing

I recognize as I write this book that many of you who read it are not going to be the top level executive who can make this initiative happen.

Neither am I. Nor have I ever been.

But here's the truth. You have the power and the influence to do great things within your little corner of the pond.

Everyone has the opportunity to embrace servant leadership.

Start with your immediate team. If you don't directly supervise a team, but you are part of one - talk to your supervisor and fellow team members. Get started what you can get started. The change you accomplish in your little corner will ripple out to areas around you. Even if you never cause a big organizational wave out of those ripples, you have made a difference and gained valuable leadership experience while you did so.

Here's the other truth. You also have the power and the influence to inspire a vibrant servant leader culture by example.

Be a Culture Champion.

Even if the common language never happens in your organization, recognize other Culture Champions.

Give your energy to the good stuff and it will grow.

This is the heart of servant leadership.

INSIGHTS FROM RON

The number one question I get (by far) when I speak on Creating an Authentic Servant Leadership Culture is "But what if my boss and my boss's boss and on up the ladder do not buy in?"

And the answer is - be a servant leader anyway. You may not have the management authority to change systems... yet. But right this minute... right now... you have the freedom and the moral authority to start leading in ways that are consistent with the values of authentic servant leadership. No matter how inconsistent your management systems are, or how resistant your supervisors are, they do not keep you from starting to treat people in ways that reflect that you are an authentic servant leader.

At the end of the day, servant leadership is about leading dynamic change into the future, while also nurturing healthy relationships with the people you lead and influence. There are no rules prohibiting you from leading in a way that makes it clear, as Max Lucado said, that "It is not about me. It is not about now."

EPILOGUE:
Building Your
Personal Brand

INSIGHTS FROM RON

How successful you are in creating an authentic servant leadership culture will largely depend on how authentic your reputation is – your brand. As important as all of the systems and specific strategies are in determining success, everything pales in importance compared to your personal reputation.

If people see you as authentically committed to authentic servant leadership values, they will be drawn to you and your vision for the future. But if they see you as a phony, all of the systems and strategies in the world will not help you succeed.

May you have the courage to authentically walk the talk of servant leadership, and may you never forget that "It is not about me. It is not about now."

This book addresses building brands and creating cultures of authentic servant leadership in organizations.

Yet we know that leaders cannot implement the cultural shift we outline unless they themselves are authentic servant leaders. Day in and day out, their personal brand must fully and consistently embody the character traits of a servant leader.

This is a good place to mention that just as there may be a difference between how you think your team perceives your organization and the way they actually do, there may also be a difference in how your co-workers and direct reports perceive your leadership.

This is also a good place to remind you that when I speak of leadership, please frame it as situational as well as positional. In other words, even if your role does not inherently put you in a position of leadership, your personal brand will be built on the way you conduct yourself when situations arise for you to be a leader.

*With or without title and authority.

An important distinction before we dive in. There is a difference between developing a personal brand and developing a professional development plan.

A professional development plan is about the skills or expertise, the responsibilities or experiences, you need to grow in your career. The conferences, certifications, projects and accomplishment list.

A personal brand is the set of human characteristics others associate with you as both a person and a professional. These are the soft skills that differentiate a good administrator from a great leader.

STEP 1: DETERMINE DESIRED PERSONAL BRAND

How do you want others to perceive you? This is a tricky exercise because you must be aspirational without being unrealistic.

There are some things that are just innate to our personalities. Not everyone has the ability to be a gregarious, outgoing spokesperson just like not everyone has the natural inclination to observe and analyze.

I am a neurotic planner. And I don't do kinda. If there's a way to make a to-do list for something, I've made one. It would be completely unrealistic for me to decide I want to be spontaneous. Truthfully, it is also really hard for me to not be in charge. But I am working on being less obsessed with controlling every detail. I decided that I want my personal brand to reflect flexibility and rolling with the punches more than "freaks out if laminated itinerary goes missing." (true story)

Know yourself.

As you make the list of no more than 5 -7 human characteristics you want associated with your personal brand, know yourself. Be authentic about who you are at your core. That doesn't mean you can't develop the emotional intelligence or soft skills you may need to change perception, but it could mean that doing so will take a great deal of mindfulness and intention.

If you are committed to being a servant leader, ensure that some representation of Greenleaf's 12 characteristics of a servant leader are included in your inventory.

STEP 2: GET FEEDBACK

This is going to be very familiar at this point. Make a wide ranging list of characteristics that could be associated with your personal brand. Make sure to include the qualities you selected as your desired personal brand as well as some of the descriptors for traits you know you may struggle with.

The list could look something like this:

Authentic	Caring
Puts People First	Unreliable
Honest	Approachable
Hard-working	Inconsistent
Trustworthy	Acceptable
Reliable	Stale
Courteous	Cutting Edge
Covert	Difficult
Innovative	Ineffective
Dedicated	Elitist
Responsible	Resourceful
Dishonest	Friendly
Service-oriented	Rude
Lazy	Forward thinking

Once you have a characteristic list compiled, seek out feedback. Be very careful who you include in this process. You want peers, subordinates and supervisors. You want a mix of genders, ages and leadership levels. More than anything, you want honesty.

To make this less awkward, print the list out. Have an open discussion face to face with those you choose to approach. Tell them the value and importance of honest feedback and how their support in this exercise will allow you to determine what steps you may need to take to become the leader you want to be. Leave them with the list and give them a completely anonymous way to return it to you.

STEP 3: YOUR PERSONAL BRAND ROADMAP

You are going to do the same exact process here that I walked you through in the organizational section of the book.

List the characteristics you identified as your desired personal brand on the right-hand side of the page.

Determine the equal number of most frequently circled characteristics you received as feedback.

This is your current personal brand.

Draw a straight line where you have matches.

Draw a dotted line where the characteristics are close and may just require some refining.

Circle any characteristics from the feedback that are unflattering and/or definitely need to change.

Star the characteristics on the right side that are not at all represented on the left side.

Now take the time to reflect without beating yourself up. Reach out to the people you trust and ask for feedback.

Your goal should be to be conscious of the actions that contribute to the circled attributes you want to change as well as the actions that create the attributes you want to embody.

This change in your personal brand has to happen one day at a time. You will have to remain mindful of your words, of your reactions and even your lack of action.

Let's revisit a section from the beginning of this book in a new light.

Here are the key elements of building a personal brand:

Brand voice

The way you talk, when you talk and the words you choose all contribute to your brand. Your writing ability and style are also a factor here.

Brand positioning

How do you differentiate yourself from others? What makes you unique? How do you express that in a way that doesn't come off as humblebrag?

Brand standards

At first this may seem the least relevant, but I argue in many ways it is key. Have you ever heard the term dress for the job you want, not the one you have? In this case, embody the brand you want in your appearance and the appearance of your work product.

Brand placement

I love this part of personal branding, particularly in the global and digital age. Is the person you are on social media reflective of the personal brand you desire? Don't put yourself in a situation or in a position that isn't consistent with the personal brand you are trying to establish.

Brand priorities

What do you need to realign to establish the personal brand you desire? What is most important?

Brand consistency

Again, as far as I'm concerned, consistency is the golden rule of branding. There is no more certain doom for a brand, including a personal one, than lack of consistency.

My very best to you as you work to make servant leadership your brand.

Know that at times the pressure of society to accomplish and your own personal ambitions to move ahead may seem in drastic contrast to being an authentic servant leader.

In those times, remember that if it is about you – you aren't being a servant leader. Check your ego. Release the need for the gold star.

Instead, return to the core characteristics of your personal brand.

Focus on staying authentic to the leader you want to be, even if it means you aren't immediately recognized.

Life, both personally and professionally, is about leaving something good behind.

Acknowledgements

To Brother Ray, Don, Dick, Joanne, Dean and Amy - the servant leaders who first showed me the path to public service.

To Ryan, Gina and Dan for their insights.

To Ron for the amazing opportunity to collaborate on a topic where we share such passion.

To my Mom and Dad – my first and best examples of selfless, humble servant leadership.

To Mark – my coach & my hero

To Jake & Quinn - may you be filled with loving kindness, may you be well, may you be peaceful and at ease, may you be happy. You are my something good.

Stacy

CPSIA information can be obtained
at www.ICGtesting.com
Printed in the USA
LVHW091609230519
618696LV00032B/14/P

9 781644 383124